GRACING FAVOR

…the two leaved gate for unparalleled Greatness!

TOBE MOMAH M.D.

ISBN 978-1-959895-51-0 (paperback)
ISBN 978-1-959895-50-3 (ebook)

Copyright © 2022 by Tobe Momah M.D.

All rights reserved. No part of this publication may be reproduced, distributed, or transmitted in any form or by any means, including photocopying, recording, or other electronic or mechanical methods without the prior written permission of the publisher.

Printed in the United States of America

WESTPOINT
PRINT AND MEDIA

CONTENTS

Dedication 5
Acknowledgements 7
Foreword 9
Preface 11

Part I: Principles Of Gracing Favor 15
Chapter One: Defining Gracing Favor 17
Chapter Two: Dispensations Of Gracing Favor 23
Chapter Three: Desire For Gracing Favor 30
Chapter Four: Discovering Gracing Favor 37
Chapter Five: Dimensions Of Gracing Favor 44
Chapter Six: Duplicitous Thoughts On Gracing Favor .. 50
Chapter Seven: Dividends Of Gracing Favor 57

Part II: Profiles In Gracing Favor 63
Chapter Eight: David: A Profile In Gracing Favor 65
Chapter Nine: Samuel: A Profile In Gracing Favor 73
Chapter Ten: Ezra: A Profile In Gracing Favor 79
Chapter Eleven: Mary: A Profile In Gracing Favor 85
Chapter Twelve: Joseph: A Profile In Gracing Favor 90

Chapter Thirteen: Esther: A Profile In Gracing Favor.... 97

Chapter Fourteen: Noah: A Profile In Gracing Favor... 105

Chapter Fifteen: Nehemiah: A Profile In
    Gracing Favor 112

Chapter Sixteen: Daniel: A Profile In Gracing Favor.... 119

Chapter Seventeen: Job: A Profile In Gracing Favor..... 125

Chapter Eighteen: Jesus: A Profile In Gracing Favor.... 131

Part III: Pathways To Gracing Favor 137

Chapter Nineteen: Shout 139

Chapter Twenty: Stand... 146

Chapter Twenty-One: Sight... 152

Chapter Twenty-Two: Supplications 158

Chapter Twenty-Three: Surrender 166

Chapter Twenty-Four: Situate.. 172

Chapter Twenty-Five: Service 179

Chapter Twenty-Six: Shed Love 186

Chapter Twenty-Seven: Swiftness.................................. 192

Chapter Twenty-Eight: Sincerity 198

Chapter Twenty-Nine: Stirrings..................................... 205

Part IV: Conclusion 211

Chapter Thirty: The A To Z Of Gracing Favor............ 213

DEDICATION

I dedicate this book to my mother, Chief (Mrs) Christy Ifeoma Momah. An amazon, quintessential champion, celebrated mother in Israel, advocate for the weak, defender of the disenfranchised, and supporter of the small she has over the years been labelled in our family as the *incurable optimist*.

No matter how dark the circumstances are, my mother always stands tall in hope and is never short of great expectations. Her phrases are typically short, but profound. She taught us early in life that *failure is a bastard, and success has many fathers*. She speaks from the heart, and never fails to speak the truth in love.

She taught my wife and I how to appreciate one's spouse by how she dotted on my father, late General (Dr.) Sam Momah, for fifty one years. She never stopped telling who ever cared to listen rippling stories of their courtship, marriage, and raising five children through the turmoil of war, coups, politics, and businesses.

Now, at Seventy-five years of age she is like the wine that gets better with age! Her acumen is sharp, her mien supportive, her vision broad, and her scope all-accepting to all that come to her. She is the proverbial succor, reputed refuge, and trusted companion that leaves those who come into her presence with a smile on the face, and a pep in their step.

Her life espouses the ideals of ***Gracing Favor.*** The philanthropy, forgiveness, passion, and rest she exhibits is proof of Gracing Favor. Mummy, I celebrate you and pronounce you blessed in Jesus name. May your days be long, and your years robust in Jesus name.

ACKNOWLEDGEMENTS

God inspired this book. He gave the words and allowed me to put them in print. It, however, would not have been possible without some invaluable assets along the journey who saw value in it and spurred me on. More than anyone else, my wife of eighteen years, Rita, provided a setting that encouraged and sharpened me to write. She has been my co-traveler on our unusual journey of ***Gracing Favor***, and even more so has been a ringside witness to the Glory fulfilled as a result.

My Church, Miracle Temple Evangelistic Church, Jackson Mississippi, and my pastors, Bishop and first lady Kenneth and Dorothy Preston, gave me a limitless platform to teach on this subject over a period of three months. Their encouragement enabled me to keep adding to the material until it became reality. I, also, want to thank members of the ministry I superintend, Faith and Power Ministries, for their support and loyalty during this adventure. Their prayers and concerted efforts throughout the writing of this book were extra-ordinary.

My parents, late General (Dr.) and Mrs. Momah encouraged my writing to no end. From enrolling me in a computer school program, and paying for all my education home and abroad, they have inspired me again and again to always go for my dreams and keep hope alive. They, alongside my siblings - Amaka, Ada, Emeka and Nkem and their spouses - have supported me in more ways than one and my heart overflows with appreciation to them.

Finally, I want to thank the body of Christ. They have embraced this gospel message of *Gracing Favor* and afforded me the opportunity, via in person preaching, livestream media, radio and/or television to air and teach the principles I have elucidated in this book. I trust that what you have made happen to me God will make happen for you multiple times over, in Jesus name! Amen.

FOREWORD

In a world filled with instabilities, crises, and chaos, it can sometimes seem impossible to maintain your peace. But in these despairing times, God will send his servants as a beacon of hope, and anoint them to deliver a message that destroys bondages and removes burdens from the lives of His people. I believe that Dr. Tobe Momah is one of those servants, and *Gracing Favor* is that message.

This powerful message is conveyed in the book of Esther—a dramatic account of God's special purpose for His people, His timeless love, the unsurpassed favor His presence brings, and the courage and responsibility that comes along with it. Esther—though a Jewish woman in a foreign land—became the Queen of Persia because of God's gracing favor after Queen Vashti was deposed from her throne. In Esther 2:17, the Bible says "*...the king loved Esther above all the women, and she obtained **grace** and **favor** in his sight more than all the virgins; so that he set the royal crown upon her head, and made her queen instead of Vashti.*"

As you read this book, you will learn that the anointing of God may bring you to the palace, but it is His grace and favor that will sustain you upon arriving there. The ascendancy of Haman, the king's official, was never a threat to Esther, her Uncle (Mordecai), or their

Jewish nation, because God had already determined to take what the enemy meant for evil and work it together for their good. And when God promotes, no Haman can demote!

Just as God adequately equipped Esther for the call upon her life for such a unique moment in history, God has also equipped you with everything you need for your "such a time as this." When death threatened Esther, she opened her mouth with God's instruction even when it was risky to do so. This is the example that every believer should follow. Keep silent no more! She was vindicated, and so shall you be as you listen, believe and unashamedly broadcast this message of God's *Gracing Favor* to His glory in Jesus name!

Jennifer Baird
Senior Pastor
Jackson Revival center, Jackson MS

PREFACE

I woke up from sleep with those two words – *Gracing favor* - emblazoned before my subconscious. I had received a visitation from God while asleep, with marching orders to tell the world about this realm of *Gracing favor* that God was unleashing upon the Church in the last days.

In the vision, I heard God describe *Gracing Favor* as a last day key to bringing unparalleled greatness to His Church. He explained that the key difference with **Gracing favor**, as compared to other messages on favor or grace, is that it is a twin combination that yields formerly unseen heights of divine glory.

He, also, emphasized, that it is a dispensation where the Church will have the *Favor to get* and *grace to stand* no matter what odds they face. Over the years, the Church has been besieged with a hyper grace message, with many of those propagating it falling, failing, and faltering to stand despite God outpouring of favor upon them.

These ones have opened only one side of God's end time gates. *Gracing favor*, to the contrary, is a two leaved gate that God opens for His people (Isaiah 45:1-3). These two leaved gates are the access way to Kingly palaces, and consist of God's power twins of Grace and favor that turn gory into glory, and shame into shining.

In Isaiah 60:10-11, the Lord says "*...the sons of strangers shall build up thy walls, and their kings shall minister unto thee: for in my wrath I smote thee, but in **my favor** have I had **mercy** on thee. Therefore **thy gates** shall be open continually; they shall not be shut day nor night; that men may bring unto thee the forces of the Gentiles, and that their kings may be brought.*"

The gates, mentioned in Isaiah 60:11, are the twin gates of favor and mercy (or grace) and are the gates that "*...give thee the treasures of darkness, and hidden riches of secret places,...*" (Isaiah 45:3). *Gracing Favor* is a last day word for the body of Christ, and especially for those want progress with power, anointing with acceleration, and favor with fruitfulness.

Gracing favor is the kindler to the life you only once dreamed about, and leads to open gates of increase and invincibility. It (*gracing favor*) will cause "*...people* (to)... *be all righteous*: (and) *they shall inherit the land for ever,* (be) *the branch of* (His) *planting,* (and) *the work of* (His) *hands, that* (He) *may be glorified*" (Isaiah 60:21). Happy reading, in Jesus mighty name.

Gracing Favor is Favor to Get, and Grace to Stand!

—Tobe Momah M.D.

PART I

Principles of Gracing Favor

- Defining Gracing Favor
- Dispensations of Gracing Favor
- Desire for Gracing Favor
- Discovering Gracing Favor
- Dimensions of Gracing Favor
- Duplicitous thoughts on Gracing Favor
- Dividends of Gracing Favor

The Tragedy of our Time are not unanswered or unoffered prayers, but unoffered lives!

—Tobe Momah M.D.

CHAPTER ONE

DEFINING GRACING FAVOR

> *"...in my wrath I smote thee, but in my **favor** have I had **mercy** on thee. Therefore **thy gates** shall be open continually; they shall not be shut day nor night; that men may bring unto thee the forces of the Gentiles, and that their kings may be brought. For the nation and kingdom that will not serve thee shall perish; yea, those nations shall be utterly wasted"* (Isaiah 60:11-12).

There is a realm of favor the last-day Church will enter that prior generations would only have dreamt about. It is the realm called ***Gracing favor.*** This is a two leaved gate that guarantees the Church will have *"for* (their) *shame...double; and for confusion they shall rejoice in their portion:* (and) *therefore in their land they shall possess the double..."* (Isaiah 61:7).

This latter day Church will taste double for their trouble! In Proverbs 16:15, the wise man said "*in the light of the king's countenance is life; and **his favor** is as **a cloud of the latter rain.**"* That latter rain cloud of favor is earmarked to surround the last day Church.

According to James 5:7-9, "*...the husbandman waiteth for the precious fruit of the earth, and hath long patience for it, until he receive the **early and latter rain**. Be ye also patient; stablish your hearts: for the coming of the Lord draweth nigh.*" The merging of the latter and former rain are synonymous with the coming of the Lord, and since "*...favor is as a cloud of latter rain...*" (Proverbs 16:15) the signature of the last day Church will be unparalleled favor.

These ones, like Queen Esther, go from nonentity to notoriety. In Esther 2:17, the Bible says "*...the king loved Esther above all the women, and she obtained **grace** and **favor** in his sight more than all the virgins; so that he set the royal crown upon her head, and made her queen instead of Vashti.*"

The reign of Queen Esther unveiled God's glory in an unsurpassed manner for the Jews (see Esther 8:17), but it was predicated on the platform of *gracing favor*. It was no wonder, therefore, that Queen Esther reigned perpetually (Esther 9:31-32) where her predecessors had been deposed un ceremonially. Gracing favor is the *favor to get* with a *grace to stand* nonetheless.

FROM LOCAL TO GLOBAL

The two leaved gates of Grace and Favor are why the heathen king Cyrus broke barriers and became a global colossus. In Isaiah 45:1-3, the Bible says "*...to his anointed, to Cyrus, whose right hand I have holden, to* *subdue nations before him; and I will loose the loins of kings, to open before him **the two leaved gates** and the gates shall not be shut; I will go before thee, and make the crooked places straight: I will break in pieces the gates of brass, and cut in sunder the bars of iron: And I will give thee the treasures of darkness, and hidden riches of secret places...."*

It was because God had given favor (loosened loins) and grace (by holding his right hand) that Cyrus conquered all of the known world in his time, and brought Israel back to Jerusalem. These gates he was given access to were kingly gates that opened the doors to limitless resources, and that is what the end time Church has been earmarked for if they embrace the message of gracing favor.

In Psalm 44:1-3, the Psalmist states that God "... *didst drive out the heathen with* (His) *hand, and plantedst them;...and cast them out. For they got not the land in possession by their own sword, neither did their own arm save them: but* (His) ***right hand, and thine arm**, and **the light of thy countenance**, because thou hadst a **favor** unto them.*"

When Grace and favor collide, open gates of limitless resources and blessings are inevitable. These lands the Israelites got were not ordinary lands, but "...*a land for which* (they) *did not labor, and cities which* (they) *built not, and* (they) *dwell in them;* (and) *of the vineyards and olive yards which* (they) *planted not do* (they) *eat*" (Joshua 24:13). If they got this by favor, imaging what *gracing favor* will do for you and I in these last days!

THE ORIGINS OF GRACE AND FAVOR

Both favor and grace, in the original Greek, are interpreted from the Greek word *Charis*. It means to be acceptable, merciful, express kindness, or receive benefits by divine ability. Favor and Grace are a God thing, and not something merited, deserved, or accrued at human cost. Another definition is derived from the Hebrew Word, ***Chinnam,*** and it means **without cost or cause**.

The Gracing Favor of God is a God-orchestrated last day move of God to prove the veracity of His Word in the lives of His people. Grace and Favor are divine in origin, and not man-made or human orchestrated. In Psalm 106:4, the Psalmist prayed *"remember me, O LORD, with the **favor** that thou bearest unto thy people:…."*

Gracing favor is not because of hard work, but because it is the due season for manifestation! As the Psalmist decreed, God "*…shalt arise, and have **mercy** upon Zion: for the time to **favor** her, yea, the set time, is come*" (Psalm 102:13). Now is the set time for God to favor the Church, and show her mercy (otherwise called Grace). Get ready; your set time for Gracing Favor has come.

THE BROOKLYN YEARS

In 2005, straight out of the mission fields of Gimbie, Ethiopia and with little American clinical experience, God miraculously gave me a place to train as a General Surgeon at the Brooklyn Hospital, New York. It was, however, a non-designated preliminary position and there were no guarantees from my *Good Samaritan* (Dr Carryl) that I would be offered a permanent position (amidst the high attrition pyramidal surgical residency programs were reputed for).

As the preliminary non-designated two year position in General Surgery was winding down, my department Chair told me I was being considered for a categorical position but that would mean going back to first year and starting the five to six year program all over again. I was on a work permit that limited my training to seven years maximum, and in order to avoid immigration complications, I began exploring alternatives.

Unknown to me, the Family Medicine residents at the same hospital (particularly their chief Residents) had observed my work ethic and recommended me to the program director for a position in Family Medicine. I interviewed with them, was offered a position, and went on to graduate top of my class. Years later, at a national Family Medicine conference in San Antonio Texas, I asked one of those chief residents why they recommended me to their program director. She said they just liked the way I responded to them. I was not obtrusive, or abrasive but spoke calmly and respectfully to them.

Eventually, I went on to become a board certified family and Obesity physician, who served as the Medical Director of one of the largest community health center in Louisiana for five years. I am currently faculty and an Associate professor at a United States Medical school, and believe all I have achieved is a product of His *Gracing Favor*. Without Him, it would have never gotten off the ground and surely would have ended in shipwreck. To Him alone be all the glory!

Prayer: Make my life an evidence of your Gracing favor, in Jesus name!

Grace and Favor are the Hinges on which Wide Doors Open!

—Tobe Momah M.D.

CHAPTER TWO

DISPENSATIONS OF GRACING FAVOR

> "*In the light of the king's countenance is life; and his **favor** is as a **cloud of the latter rain**"* (Proverbs 16:15).

One of the characteristics of the last days Church is an avalanche of God's Gracing Favor upon her. In Proverbs 16:15, the wise man said "*in the light of the king's countenance is life; and **his favor** is as a **cloud of the latter rain**.*" Whenever the term *latter rain* is utilized in the Bible, as in James 5:7-9, it connotes last days' timing.

In Joel 2:23,28 Prophet Joel said "*be glad then, ye children of Zion, and rejoice in the LORD your God: for he hath given you the former rain moderately, and he will cause to come down for you the rain, the former rain, and the **latter rain** in the first month ....And it shall come to pass afterward, that I will pour out my spirit upon all flesh.*"

The latter rain will precede the outpouring of the Holy Spirit in one last great move of the Holy Spirit. **This latter rain will be signaled by uncommon Grace and favor.** In Micah 4:1, the Lord says *"…in the last days it shall come to pass, that the mountain of the house of the LORD shall be established in the top of the mountains, and it shall be exalted above the hills; and people shall flow unto it."*

GRACE FOR GLORY

Jesus is coming back for a glorious Church; He said in Ephesians 5:25-27 that *"…Christ also loved the church, and gave Himself for it that He might sanctify and cleanse it with the washing of water by the word,* (and) *that He might present it to Himself a **glorious** church, not having spot, or wrinkle, or any such thing; but that it should be holy and without blemish."*

That glory, however, is due to the unparalleled Gracing Favor available in the last days. In Hebrews 12:28, the author of Hebrews says *"wherefore we receiving a kingdom which cannot be moved, let us have **grace**, whereby we may serve God acceptably with reverence and godly fear."*

No man serves God with reverence and Godly fear who does not first enter the realms of glory (see Psalm 85:9). The graciously favored Church will herald the bastion of the last day Church, and signal the greatest move of God on the earth since Pentecost. In Hosea 3:5, God said *"afterward shall the children of Israel return, and seek the LORD their God, and David their king; and shall fear the LORD and his **goodness** in the **latter days**."*

There is coming a goodness in the last days that will make even the most irreverent of men fear God! It is the realm of *gracing favor*, and it will precede His coming glory. The glorious Church will fly on the wings of these two arch-shepherds of the body of Christ and ignoring them would leave the Church hopeless, poor, irrelevant, ignored, opaque, and densely ignorant in the last days.

Grace and Favor are not accessories or luxuries for the last day Church, but essentials the Church can't live without. In Psalm 102:13-15, the Psalmist said *"thou shalt arise, and have mercy upon Zion: for the time to **favor** her, yea, the set time, is come. For thy servants take pleasure in her stones, and **favor** the dust thereof. So the heathen shall fear the name of the LORD, and all the kings of the earth thy **glory**. When the LORD shall build up Zion, he shall appear in his **glory**."*

SEIZING THE MOMENT!

The last days are a bastion of God's supernatural *gracing favor* that will unleash His unprecedented greatness of God upon her, and herald the coming of the Lord. These are also the days of the latter rain, and according to Zechariah 10:1, there is a *sine qua non* that must take place in that atmosphere.

In Zechariah 10:1, the prophet Zechariah says, *"**ask ye of the** LORD rain in the time of the **latter rain**; so the LORD shall make **bright clouds**, and give them **showers** of rain, to every one grass in the field."* Bright clouds connote favor (see Proverbs 16:15), and the showers of rain His Grace.

There must, however, be a praying Church in these last days to birth our aforementioned rain. It is the fervent prayers of the saints, for the latter rain, that cause her to shine as bright clouds. The signature of the Church's latter rain glory is *gracing favor*. It will, however, be accessed by supernatural supplications (see Zechariah 12:10).

The word *supplication* is the Greek word *Deomai*, and it means to pray for a specific need, and make a heartfelt petition that arises out of a deep personal need. *Gracing favor* is not wished for, wondered at, or worried for. Rather, it must be warred for! The manifestation of the after effects of that prayer are seen in Zechariah 11:1; it says, "*open **thy doors**, O Lebanon, that the fire may devour thy cedars….*"

PROPHECY FROM AZUSA STREET

The Azusa Street revival birthed the modern-day Pentecostal-themed Church in 1905. It was headlined by leaders such as William Seymour and Charles Parham. As the revival was winding down in 1913, both men gave prophecies from two different locations stating that in one hundred years' time, there will be a *greater-than-Azuza* Street revival in America.

Following their prophecies, an Evangelist with the Assemblies of God Maria Woodworth-Etter, prophesied in December 1913, that "*there will be a greater move of God in the next one hundred years, the glory of which has never been seen on the surface of the earth.*"

A hundred and five years later, these prophecies are being fulfilled all around the world. Africa, for example, has gone from a less than five percent Christian population in 1900 to more than fifty-five percent in 2010.[1] It is now projected as the fastest growing religion on the continent, with an estimated 700 million adherents projected in 2030.[1]

It was on Africa's poverty-ridden soils that a ministry, Christ For All Nations (CFAN), celebrated a harvest of seventy five million souls in a little more than forty years. Other nation states such as Singapore, South Korea, and China have seen a great turning to the Lord Jesus Christ. The landmark *Yoido full Gospel* Church was at its peak a million-member Church, and the underground Church in China is nearly a hundred million strong.

Even the 10-40 window, a hotbed of Islamic irredentists who restrict the preaching of the gospel, is opening up. In Indonesia, the largest Moslem nation on earth, there are Churches of ten thousand and growing. In the Middle East, recent *Arab Spring* movements have allowed for more-tolerant and western-leaning governments to arise which embrace the *ethos* of Christianity.

It may not be *Eureka* yet, but the signs of a gathering of great clouds of revival are coming. A replacement of the old-guard with young visionary leadership, including the likes of Paul Enenche, Brian Houston, Joel Osteen, Christine Caine, and Priscilla Shearer are creating a more relevant Church today. With increased interest in social causes and injustice, this new generation seems

---

[1] Tolerance and tension: Islam and Christianity in Sub-Saharan Africa. Pew Research center religion and public life. April 15, 2010

like a new sound designed to break the old cycle of denominationalism and legalism.

Prayer: Baptize me with the oil for Gracing Favor, in Jesus name!

The Largest Room in an individual is the Room for Improvement

—Bruce Wilkinson
(Author/Preacher/Teacher)

CHAPTER THREE

DESIRE FOR GRACING FAVOR

*"A good name is rather to be chosen than great riches, and **loving favor** rather than silver and gold"* (Proverbs 22:1).

There must be a desire for *gracing favor* before it can deliver for the individual! This generation has not been taught to love grace and favor, and as a result are forlorn, frustrated and fearful of the world around them. In Matthew 5:6, Jesus said *"blessed are they which do hunger and thirst after righteousness: for they shall be filled."*

Favor is a veritable weapon, but only when it is wanted! It is a weapon against shame, but only when shame is despised and Favor is desired. In Hebrews 12:2, the Bible tells us Jesus is *"...the author and finisher of our faith; who for the joy that was set before him endured the cross, **despising the shame**, and is set down at the right hand of the throne of God."*

Desiring the favor of God is the reason for the obliteration of shame. When a thirteen year old girl, Mary, was found to be with child in Luke 1 and was about to be ashamed and assaulted by the mob, the angel appeared to Mary and called her "*...highly favored...*" (Luke 1:28). Instead of shrugging off the Angel's invitation, as a typical teenager, Mary said "*...behold the handmaid of the Lord; be it unto me according to thy word...*" (Luke 1:38).

She desired it (high favor), rather than despised it and it manifested in her life! This generation's mindset of shame needs to be replaced with a love for favor. The wise man said "*...loving favor is better than silver and Gold*" (Proverbs 22:1). Too many people will rather live in shame than despise it, like Jesus did in Hebrews 12:2.

If Mary had lived ashamed, rather than accept God's favor, she would never have become the birth mother of Jesus. Her desire trumped her duty as a fiancée, and her passion broke the protocol for betrothed singles. Eventually, that child became "*a light to lighten the Gentiles, and the glory of thy people Israel*" (Luke 2:32).

LOVE FAVOR OR LOSE FAVOR!

There are many who don't believe they are loved. They have been abandoned or misused in the past, and as a result enter into relationships paranoid, presumptive, or parochial. The Israelites, for example, accused God of "*...hat*(ing) *us,* (and so)*...brought* (them)*...forth out of the land of Egypt, to deliver...into the hand of the Amorites, to destroy us*" (Deuteronomy 1:27).

This mindset of negativity and rejection, that makes many expect nothing from God is highly prevalent today and so defers many from their arrival at the realm of *gracing favor*. **Favor goes where it is loved, not where it is loathed!** Jesus declared in Nazareth, after he was rejected because of familiarity (Luke 4:16), that it was time to "*…to preach the acceptable year of the Lord*" (Luke 4:19).

They (the people of Nazareth) had lived in rejection, and needed a message of acceptance from God to gain the approval of men. In Romans 14:17-18, Apostle Paul said "*…the kingdom of God is not meat and drink; but righteousness, and peace, and joy in the Holy Ghost. For he that in these things serveth Christ is **acceptable to God, and approved of men.***"

Gracing favor is your tonic for divine acceptance. It abrogates human rejection, but requires a deep love for it to manifest. That is why the wise man, in Ephesians 1:5-6, said God "*having predestinated us unto the adoption of children by Jesus Christ to himself, according to the good **pleasure** of his will, to the praise of the glory of his grace, wherein he hath made us **accepted in the beloved**.*"

HIS ATTITUDE FOR MY HIGHEST ALTITUDE

One day of favor is greater than a lifetime of labor. God's attitude is not to jettison or judge favor, but rather love favor (Proverbs 22:1). This attitude of loving favor is a lifestyle in the kingdom. It is a kingdom attribute to be accepted by God, and expect approval of man as a result.

In Ephesians 1:6, Apostle Paul said "*…he hath made us accepted in the beloved*" and in Proverbs 16:6-7, the wise man said "*by **mercy** (or favor) and truth (or grace) iniquity* *is purged: and by the fear of the LORD* men depart from evil. When a man›s ways *please the LORD, he maketh even his enemies to be at peace with him."*

It is undeniable that some people will dislike you (see Luke 21:16-17), but they don't have permission to deny you of heaven's will for your life! The greatest lesson, therefore, for today's Church is to have an attitude shift where believers know that amidst the worst rejection, God can still favor them with supernatural grace.

In Luke 21:28, while chronicling the last days, Jesus said "...*when these things begin to come to pass, then look up, and lift up your heads; for your redemption draweth nigh."* The believer must have an *acceptance attitude*, instead of a *victim volition*, to reach his or her highest altitude.

For example, after "...*the children of Israel did according to the word of Moses...*(and) *borrowed of the Egyptians jewels of silver, and jewels of gold, and raiment*" (Exodus 12:35), the "...*LORD gave the people favor in the sight of the Egyptians, so that they lent unto them such things as they required. And they spoiled the Egyptians*" (Exodus 12:36).

These Israelites, who had been slaves to the Egyptians for 430 years, did not despise *gracing favor*, but rather embraced it when the opportunity to acquire wealth from the Egyptians came (see Exodus 3:21-22, Exodus 11:2-3). They took heed to Moses word, and spoiled the Egyptians (Exodus 12:36), while still their slaves and subordinates.

Favor is not fair, yet it is God's will for the Church. In the midst of last day opportunity and increase, the Church must love favor fervently and grow in grace greatly. It is this type of attitude that births the altitude for divine blessings. That is why, in Micah 4:1-2, God says "*in the last days it shall come to pass, that the mountain of the house of the LORD shall be established in the top of the mountains, and it shall be exalted above the hills; and people shall **flow** unto it. And many nations shall come, and say, come, and let us go up to the mountain of the LORD, and to the house of the God of Jacob; and he will teach us of his ways, and we will walk in his paths: for the law shall go forth of Zion, and the word of the LORD* from Jerusalem."

CHAIRS FROM CHINA

A member of Dunamis International Gospel Center (DIGC), Abuja Nigeria made a pledge to buy all the chairs for the new 100,000 capacity auditorium. He was a successful businessman, but did not have sufficient funds at that time to purchase the needed chairs at their current cost. Nonetheless, he had the desire to do so, and so believed God for the funds to do so.

As the DIGC glory dome in Abuja got roofed, and chairs were about to be installed this gentleman boarded a plane headed to Asia to find out if he could purchase the Chairs at a decreased price. He normally flew first class, but after his layover in Dubai, he was moved to business class because the airline had overbooked the first class flight cabin.

The Holy Spirit told him not to protest, and just before the plane took off the gentleman seated next to him asked him why he was going to China. After telling him his mission, and the cause he was supporting, the man introduced himself as the managing director of the largest chair making factory in the Philippines.

By the end of the trip, the gentleman had offered to sell him 100,000 seats of the utmost quality at 50% the cost he would have purchased them in China. At the commissioning of the DIGC glory dome, all 100,000 seats had been supplied and this one member had fulfilled his promise to God. His seat re-configuration was a God-engineered encounter, coupled with *gracing favor*, that made fulfilling his vow possible.

Prayer: Battles of irregular favor, your time is up. Die, in Jesus name!

This Generation lives in Epileptic Favor, because they have not been taught to love favor!

—Tobe Momah M.D.

CHAPTER FOUR

DISCOVERING GRACING FAVOR

> "*He that diligently seeketh good procureth* **favor**: *but he that seeketh mischief, it shall come unto him*" (Proverbs 11:27).

The desire for Gracing Favor must not just stop there; it must be coupled with knowledge on how to discover it as well. Many have a desire but leave it at that, and end up without *gracing favor* because they do not know how to discover *gracing favor*.

In Proverbs 18:1, the wise man says "*through desire a man, having separated himself, seeketh and intermeddleth with all wisdom.*" That means that desire alone is not enough. If there is a desire for anything, it must be backed up with diligence, dedication, and desperation to birth discovery.

To discover gracing favor, there must be seeking by the individual that is diligent and directed. That is why, in Proverbs 11:27, the wise man says *"he that diligently seeketh good procureth favour: but he that seeketh mischief, it shall come unto him."* What you diligently pursue will inadvertently follow you, whether good or bad.

The word, *good,* as used in Proverbs 11:27 is the Greek word *towb* and it means beautiful, and cheerful. Pursuing peace, joy, and righteousness with diligence and in a timely manner causes *gracing favor* to manifest. That is why the wise man counseled the people of his day to never let the Word of God go, but keep it in view always.

He said, in Proverbs 3:1-4 *"my son, forget not my law; but let thine heart keep my commandments: For length of days, and long life, and peace, shall they add to thee. Let not mercy and truth forsake thee: bind them about thy neck; write them upon the table of thine heart: So shalt thou find **favor** and **good understanding** in the sight of God and man."*

THE PRAYER FOR FAVOR

In Nehemiah 2, the prayers for favor by Nehemiah – a cup bearer to King Artaxerxes – are highlighted. In Nehemiah 2:4-5, he said *"…I prayed to the God of heaven. And I said unto the king, If it please the king, and if thy servant have found **favor** in thy sight, that thou wouldest send me unto Judah, unto the city of my fathers' sepulchres, that I may build it."*

The prayer of favor can change in a second what a lifetime of labor failed to accomplish! The prayer for favor can settle issues that have gone unraveled for centuries. Nehemiah's prayers kick started the beginning of the end of the disgrace the rubbish around Israel's wall had generated (Nehemiah 1:3-4).

He (Nehemiah) desired change, but also diligently sought Jerusalem's change by prayer and hard work. That is why, in Nehemiah 4:9, though the enemies of Israel "...*conspired all of them together to come and to fight against Jerusalem, and to hinder* (them), *nevertheless* (they)... *made...prayer unto our God, and set a watch against them day and night, because of them.*"

What the Israelites had endured for more than 70 years, resolved in a space of fifty two days (Nehemiah 6:15) because a man prayed and diligently sought the good of Israel. It was the prayer of Nehemiah, in Nehemiah 1:11, saying "*o LORD, I beseech thee, let now thine ear be attentive to the prayer of thy servant, and to the prayer of thy servants, who desire to fear thy name: and prosper, I pray thee, thy servant this day, and grant him **mercy** (favor) in the sight of this man*" that changed everything.

The prayer for favor ignores limitations and causes the super to be put on the natural. It breaks barriers, and establishes outpourings. As a result of Nehemiah's petition, the Bible says "...*the king granted me* (all my request), *according to the good hand of my God upon me*" (Nehemiah 2:8b).

When David wanted divine favor, he "...*in treated* (God's) ***favor*** with (his) *whole heart...*" (Psalm 119:58). The aftermath was supernatural *gracing favor* on King David, such that God called him "...*a man after His own heart...*" (1 Samuel 13:14), and Stephen described him as David "*who found favor before God, and desired to find a tabernacle for the God of Jacob*" (Acts 7:46).

FAITH FOR FAVOR AND FRUITFULNESS

Another key to discovering *gracing favor* is the Word of God. In Proverbs 13:15-16, the wise man said "*good understanding giveth favor: but the way of transgressors is hard. Every prudent man dealeth with knowledge:....*" There is no understanding outside the primacy of the Word of God (Proverbs 3:1-5), and that understanding is the key to favor, and fruitfulness.

God looked on Israel in favor and the mountains exploded with men and resources. In Ezekiel 35, the mountains devoured men but when favor came in Ezekiel 36 they developed men and resources into fruitfulness. Favor is God's manifest mercy for a people, and it causes a windfall of fruitfulness.

In Ezekiel 36:9-11, the Lord said "*...I am for you, and I will turn unto you, and ye shall be tilled and sown: And I will multiply men upon you, all the house of Israel, even all of it: and the cities shall be inhabited, and the wastes shall be builded: And I will multiply upon you man and beast; and they shall increase and bring fruit: and I will settle you after your old estates, and will do better unto you than at your beginnings....*"

When favor stops, labor starts but when favor is present, multiplication that causes prosperity is inevitable. In Acts 2:46-47, the Bible says the early disciples "*...continuing daily with one accord in the temple, and breaking bread from house to house,* (and who) *did eat their meat with gladness and singleness of heart,* (were) *praising God, and having **favor** with all the people....*"

They grew in favor, in the early Church, and comfort - not commotion - was the result. This comfort of the Holy Spirit brought inspiration, not perspiration, so much so that *"...the churches* (had) *rest throughout all Judaea and Galilee and Samaria, and were edified; and **walking in the fear of the Lord**, and in the **comfort of the Holy Ghost**, were multiplied"* (Acts 9:31).

Walking in the *Zoe* life of God, is the *sine-qua-non* for favor! It turns night into day, and mourning into joy! Take hold of the spirit of the Word, and God will grant you His *gracing favor*. In Psalm 30:5, the Psalmist said "*...in his* (God's) *favor is life..."* and in Proverbs 16:15, the wise man adds that *"in the light of the king's countenance is life; and his favor is as a cloud of the latter rain."*

BILLY'S BIG BREAK

Evangelist Billy Graham (1918 – 2018) was holding tent crusades in Los Angeles, California in October 1949 with very little public attention. One fateful morning, however, William Randolph Hearst was jogging past the Billy Graham Evangelistic Association when he noticed the congregation streaming in and out of the fairly sized tent and sent a two word directive to his newspapers (including New York Times and Los Angeles Times) to *puff Graham*.

That two word directive led to Billy Graham been splashed across the front pages of east and west coast dailies, and soon after a media circus including Hollywood celebrities descended on his evangelistic rallies. His meteoric rise never came down. He went on to preach to more than 2 billion people, archetype the modern stadium-like crusade with altar call style, counsel led six United States presidents, and the first United

States preacher to have an international ministry since Moody.

He preached face to face to nearly 300 million people, and traveled to 185 countries doing the work of an evangelist. He died at the age of 99 years, and in his book *Just as I am* he states that though he never met, talked by phone, or corresponded with Mr. Hearst in his lifetime, he believes those two words *puff Graham* changed the trajectory of his ministry.

Prayer: I plug myself into the socket of divine favor and Grace, in Jesus name.

Casual Christianity always leads to Christian Casualty!

—Dr. D.K. Olukoya
General Overseer, Mountain of
Fire and Miracle Ministry

CHAPTER FIVE

DIMENSIONS OF GRACING FAVOR

*"And Jesus increased in wisdom and stature, and in **favor** with God and man"* (Luke 2:52).

Grace comes in grades and favor comes in dimensions. In Acts of the Apostles 4:33, for example, the Bible acknowledges that *"with great power gave the apostles witness of the resurrection of the Lord Jesus: and **great grace** was upon them all"* (Acts 4:33). That is the dimension the last day Church will be operating in, according to the prophetic word in Zechariah 12:10.

In that scripture, the Lord God says *"…I will pour upon the house of David, and upon the inhabitants of Jerusalem, **the spirit of grace** and of supplications: and they shall look upon me whom they have pierced, and they shall mourn for him, as one mourneth for his only son, and shall be in bitterness for him, as one that is in bitterness for his firstborn."*

The spirit of grace that causes vengeance, vindication, and victory has been poured out (see Zechariah 12:8-9), and it will ignite diverse realms of favor to dominate and enrich her environment. In Romans 5:17, the Apostle Paul says "*...by one man's offence death reigned by one; much more they which receive **abundance of grace** and of the gift of righteousness shall reign in life by one, Jesus Christ.*"

You are called to reign in these last days, but it will require an abundance of Grace (Romans 5:17) to do so. Don't settle for a mediocre, *laissez faire*, also-ran kind of grace but rather go for great and abundant grace (like the early disciples had in Acts 4:33). If you do, you will watch your enemies submit to the greatness of the power within you (see Psalm 66:3).

FROM HIGH FAVOR TO NO FAVOR

Those who operate out of hard hearts have **no favor**! In Joshua 11:20, the Bible describes Israel's enemies as "*...harden*(ing) *their hearts, that they should come against Israel in battle, that he might destroy them utterly, and that they might have **no favor**, but that he might destroy them, as the LORD commanded Moses.*"

Your softness of heart to God's stirrings guarantees the grace and favor needed to win the battles of life. A hardness of heart, on the contrary, is why marriages lose favor and Grace in each other's eyes. In Matthew 19:8, Jesus said "*...Moses because of the hardness of your hearts suffered you to put away your wives: but from the beginning it was not so.*"

On the other side of this favor spectrum, however, are the **highly favored.** Mary holds the *primus inter pares* position in this category. She was saluted by the angel as "...***highly favored***,...(and) *blessed...among women*" (Luke 1:28), and in Luke 1:30 was told by the angel to "...*fear not, Mary: for thou hast found favor with God."* The depths of your grace and the richness of your favor make for suitably assigned tasks.

Daniel and his fellow Jewish Eunuchs were called "*children in whom was no blemish, but **well favored**, and skillful in all wisdom, and cunning in knowledge, and understanding science...*" (Daniel 1:4). It was no surprise, therefore, that they ended up ten times smarter and more knowledgeable than their peers (Daniel 1:20) and the first pickings of Nebuchadnezzar and his royal court.

In Deuteronomy 33:23, Moses pronounced God's blessings upon Naphtali saying "...*O Naphtali, **satisfied with favor**, and full with the blessing of the* LORD: *possess thou the west and the south."* Until the Church is satisfied with favor, she cannot dislodge her enemies, and possess their possessions. Stop living sparsely favored, and desire, discover and be delivered into the realm of satisfied favor. It is your birthright (Psalm 106:4 and Psalm 5:12)!

INCREMENTAL FAVOR

Timing is instrumental to everything in the realm of the spirit (Ephesians 5:17-18). In Psalm 102:13-15 the Bible explains why. It says "*thou shalt arise, and have mercy upon Zion: for the **time to favor** her, yea, the set time, is come. For thy servants take pleasure in her stones, and favor the dust thereof. So the heathen shall fear the name of the* LORD, *and all the kings of the earth thy glory.*"

There is a set time for favor, and at every juncture along life's journey, there must be increase. Increase is God's signature (see Isaiah 9:7, Psalm 84:7, 2 Corinthians 3:18, and Romans 1:17), and just as Jesus "...*increased in wisdom and stature, and in favor with God and man*" (Luke 2:52) so must His body (1 Corinthians 12:27).

Divine grace and favor were not made for static existence, but as a catalyst for continuous increase. In Isaiah 49:22-23, the prophet said "...*behold, I will **lift up mine hand** to the Gentiles, and set up my standard to the people: and they shall bring thy sons in their arms, and thy daughters shall be carried upon their shoulders. And kings shall be thy nursing fathers, and their queens thy nursing mothers....*"

Until there is a lifting up, not standing still, there can be no evidence of grace and favor. This act of lifting up one's hand is synonymous with the *gracing favor* that propelled Israel out of Egypt in stupendous wealth (Exodus 12:36). In Ezekiel 20:6, the Bible says "*in the day that I lifted up mine hand unto them, to bring them forth of the land of Egypt into a land that I had espied for them, flowing with milk and honey, which is the glory of all lands.*"

MOUNTAIN OF FIRE AND MIRACLES (MFM) FOOTBALL CLUB

Dr D.K. Olukoya started the MFM ministries in the living room of his home at the National Institute of Medical Research (NIMR), Yaba, Lagos. He subsequently relocated to another location, and then to their current location in Yaba, Nigeria. As the ministry expanded, multiple means of propagating the gospel were sought and in 2013 an offer from an unlikely source threw MFM into the Nigerian professional soccer league.

The founder of Bolowotan Football Club, Toyin Gafaar, a Muslim, wanted someone reliable to maintain the work he had began on the club and so handed the football club over to the church (MFM) to manage without collecting any money in return. He said, his decision was based on the likelihood of Dr. Olukoya steering the Football Club to greater heights.

True to this testimony, within two years of the handover, this second-tier football team was promoted to the premier league division of the Nigerian soccer league, and in 2017 represented Nigeria at the continental level following a second place finish in the premier league.

The handover of a bona fide soccer team to a person of a different faith, and with no conditions attached, is unprecedented. The MFM soccer team, popularly called *Olukoya boys* now, buttress the fact that with God's grace and favor anything, including getting a football club on the free, is possible!

Prayer: I ask, O Lord, for rain in the time of the latter rain. Give me bright clouds and showers of rain in Jesus name.

Favor is more than an accessory; it is essential to the Christian life!

—Tobe Momah M.D.

CHAPTER SIX

DUPLICITOUS THOUGHTS ON GRACING FAVOR

> *"Because of the multitude of the whoredoms of the **well favored** harlot, the mistress of witchcrafts, that selleth nations through her whoredoms, and families through her witchcrafts"* (Nahum 3:4).

Favor and grace is interpreted as *charis*, in the original Greek, and it means Godly work or divine ability. Favor is a God thing, and not something merited, deserved, or accrued. It is only when the works of God are appreciated for what they are - unmerited, undeserved, and unwarranted – that the works of man can prove the veracity of the Word of God.

In Songs of Solomon 1:3, the wise man said *"because of the savor of thy good ointments thy name is as ointment poured forth, therefore do the virgins love thee."* This verse shows that it is the Holy Spirit within us (or the ointment), and not ourselves that births favor.

The word *duplicitous* means treacherous, and for the virgins to love an individual their ointment must be poured forth in transparency, earnestness, sincerity, and clarity. It cannot be a camouflage or façade, but must represent the name of Jesus and how that name has transformed them (see Romans 12:1-2).

The Apostle Paul spent time in Romans defusing these duplicitous thoughts. He asked the Church in Rome, "*...shall we continue in sin, that grace may abound? God forbid. How shall we, that are dead to sin, live any longer therein?*" (Romans 6:1-2). He then expatiated on grace, by educating the Church on the nuggets of favor and grace.

WHAT FAVOR IS NOT!

Many believers have false thoughts on favor, because there is a paucity of teachings on favor. They think **favor is not fair,** and rather expect God's system to be equitable and unanimously accepted. They balk at the idea of a man being accepted, without work and sacrifice, unaware that favor is a God thing that shows off His glory and power.

In Acts 10:34-35, Peter told Cornelius and his household "*...that God is no respecter of persons: But in every nation he that feareth him, and worketh righteousness, is **accepted with him**.*" The word *accepted* is from the Greek word *dektos*, and it means favorable. Favor does not follow the crowd, but rather follows a Christian testimony.

Other falsehoods about favor that people have is they think **favor should be frugal**. Some do not understand why favor lavishes so much on its recipients. They expect an economical, and thrifty God, but favor breaches that concept with its signature avalanche of blessings where ever it is presented.

In Psalm 44:3, the Psalmist said "...*they got not the land in possession by their own sword, neither did their own arm save them: but thy right hand, and thine arm, and the light of thy countenance, because thou hadst a **favor** unto them.*" In Joshua 24:12-13, Joshua further describes this favor gotten land.

He said, God "...*sent the hornet before you, which drave them out from before you, even the two kings of the Amorites; but not with thy sword, nor with thy bow. And* (He)...*has given you a land for which ye did not labor, and cities which ye built not, and ye dwell in them; of the vineyards and olive yards which ye planted not do ye eat.*"

That divine hornet, described in Joshua 24:12, is *gracing favor*! The land in possession was sourced by favor. It was not an ordinary land, but a land of "...*great and goodly cities, which thou buildedst not, and houses full of all good things, which thou filledst not, and wells digged, which thou diggedst not, vineyards and olive trees, which thou plantedst not;...* (Deuteronomy 6:10-11).

The Israelites got houses with ceilings that were twelve feet tall, and fully stocked with good things, and with every invaluable resource provided by favor. That is what *gracing favor* will do for you, if you come believing instead of rationalizing. In Psalm 112:3-5, the Bible says "*wealth and riches shall be in his house: and his righteousness endureth for ever. Unto the upright there ariseth light in the darkness: he is **gracious**, and full of compassion, and righteous. A good man sheweth **favor**, and lendeth: he will guide his affairs with discretion.*"

BEWARE OF THE WELL FAVORED HARLOT!

Not everything that glitters is gold. What men call well-favored a times, like in Nahum 3:4, are carefully concealed frauds fraught with hidden corruption and deadly evil. A lot of these so called favor manifestations and graciousness, are shrouded in a camouflage of corruption.

In Nahum 3:4, the Bible says *"because of the multitude of the whoredoms of the **well favored** harlot, the mistress of witchcrafts, that selleth nations through her whoredoms, and families through her witchcrafts."* The spirit of harlotry, when allowed into the Church, turns true favor into false favor.

These ones *"have a form of godliness, but deny the power thereof..."* (2 Timothy 3:5). In Revelation 2, Jesus Christ chides the Church of the last days for allowing the doctrine of the Nicolaitans (Rev 2:15), Jezebel (Rev 2:20), Balaam (Rev 2:14) in their midst. He tells them, *"remember therefore from whence thou art fallen, and repent, and do the first works; or else I will come unto thee quickly, and will remove thy candlestick out of his place, except thou repent"* (Revelation 2:5).

The duplicitous harlot appears well favored (Nahum 3:4) on the surface, but underneath are dead men's bones. Only a believer that knows that *"...satan himself is transformed into an angel of light and therefore it is no great thing if his ministers also be transformed as the ministers of righteousness..."* (2 Corinthians 11:14-15) will know the difference.

Don't follow the well favored harlot to your demise and destruction. These well favored harlot are typified in Proverbs 7 as the strange woman. They cause their victims to "*...go...after her straightway, as an ox goeth to the slaughter, or as a fool to the correction of the stocks till a dart strike through his liver* (or) *as a bird hasteth to the snare, and knoweth not that it is for his life*" (Proverbs 7:22-23).

CHRIS OKOLIE AND CATASTROPHIC OCCURRENCES!

Chris Okolie (1941 – 2007) was the first publisher of a full fledged color news magazine in Nigeria. That news magazine was called *Newbreed*, and in 1976 - after Chris returned from the Watford Institute of Technology in the United Kingdom - was launched as the flagship news magazine in Nigeria. It was proscribed by the military regime of General Olusegun Obasanjo in 1978, and remained off the shelf till 1987 when it was de-proscribed by the administration of General Babangida.

That was, however, when Chris met his ultimate waterloo in Archbishop Benson Idahosa. The charismatic tele evangelist was alleged, in 1989, by Chris Okolie's magazine to be a frontline leader of the *Ogboni* occult fraternity. Archbishop Idahosa, who had openly battled the *Ogboni* fraternity to a halt in Benin, was appalled at this *junk journalism*, and gave Chris Okolie a certain time line to retract the publication, and make a public apology, after which – if Chris Okolie refused – watch the demise of his media industry.

The rest as they say is history. Chris Okolie refused to retract the publication, or tender an apology, and from that day till the day he died (in 2007) his light was dimmed, favor obliterated, and influence abrogated. He had his news organization closed again in 1990, and this time they never returned to the newsstand. He joined the politics of the third republic in 1993, but failed in his quest for public office. He eventually died in 2007, following a motor vehicle accident that left him crippled.

A British trained journalist, Chris Okolie epitomized a life of presumption and pride. He was, by all means, a pace setting publisher, who by age 31 had started two publications namely *Newbreed* and *the President* respectively. His catastrophic end mirrors that of King Saul, who despite banning the mediums in the land (1 Samuel 28:3) ended up patronizing them (1 Samuel 28:8-25). As a result, he died as one whose "...*shield* (though)...*mighty is vilely cast away,...as though he had not been anointed with oil*" (2 Samuel 1:21).

Prayer: Baptize me with thy Gracing Favor, O Lord, in Jesus name!

The Sound you Send out will Determine the Echo you Receive!

—Tobe Momah M.D.

CHAPTER SEVEN

DIVIDENDS OF GRACING FAVOR

*"Let the elders that rule well be counted worthy of **double honor**, especially they who labor in the word and doctrine"* (1 Timothy 5:17).

Nothing represents the two-leaved gate of *Grace* and *Favor*, in the Bible, like ***Double-honor***. The Greek word for *honor* is ***tîmê***, and it means to be valuable, esteemed (of the highest degree), dignified, and of precious price. When His grace meets with divine favor, double honor is established. This double Honor, is a product of *gracing favor*, and is the two leaved gate that gives access to dignity and value.

In 2 Thessalonians 2:16-17, Apostle Paul said *"…our Lord Jesus Christ himself, and God, even our Father, which hath loved us, and hath given us everlasting consolation and good hope through **grace**, comfort your hearts, and **stablish you in every good** word and work."*

The establishment of every good work and God's word in your life stems from gracing favor, that births everlasting consolations. The Greek word for *consolation* is *paraklesis*, and it means to have a call or urging done by someone close that delivers evidence which stands up in God's court. In other words, *gracing favor* births divine help and eternal defenses.

IRRESISTIBLE FAVOR AND IRREPRESSIBLE GRACE!

There is a favor that is irresistible, and a grace that that is irrepressible! It is called ***Gracing favor***, and its essence is captured by the God of the burning bush. The Bible says "*...the angel of the LORD appeared unto him* (Moses) *in a flame of fire out of the midst of a bush: and he looked, and, behold, the bush burned with fire, and the bush was not consumed*" (Exodus 3:2).

When Moses "*...turn*(ed) *aside,* (to)*...see this great sight, why the bush is not burnt*" (Exodus 3:3), God called out to him (see Exodus 3:4). **The secret to the irresistible favor of God is the fire of the Holy Ghost**. It makes you an attention grabber anywhere you go, but first you must turn from the world and turn to Him alone.

Moses blessed Joseph with the irresistible kind of favor that the burning bush represented. In Deuteronomy 33:13-17, he told Joseph "*...blessed of the LORD* be (Joseph)*...*(Let) *the **good will of him that dwelt in the bush**,...the blessing come upon the head of Joseph, and upon the top of the head of him that was separated from his brethren. His glory is like the firstling of his bullock, and his horns are like the horns of unicorns: with them he shall push the people together to the ends of the earth:....*"

Labor without favor is only sorrow. In these last days, God's irrepressible grace and irresistible favor is designed to give you great acceleration and quickening for the blessing. In Isaiah 60:10-11, the Lord says *"… the sons of strangers shall build up thy walls, and their kings shall minister unto thee: for in my wrath I smote thee, but in **my favor** have I had mercy on thee. Therefore thy gates shall be open continually; they shall not be shut day nor night; that men may bring unto thee the forces of the Gentiles, and that their kings may be brought."*

THE FORCE OF FAVOR

Favor is power that engenders the life of God upon an individual, and even Jesus needed it for life and ministry (Luke 2:52)! In Psalm 30:5, the Psalmist said *"…His anger endureth but a moment;* (and) *in his favor is life."* In Job 10:12, this attribute of favor is further corroborated; it says *"thou hast granted me **life and favor**, and thy visitation hath preserved my spirit."*

Your glory does not depend on your labor, but on God's favor. In Psalm 44:3 and Deuteronomy 33:17 respectively, the Bible shows that the wealth displayed by a nation, or the glory exhibited by a people are not hinged on human efforts but divine excess. It is not because of hard work, but because it is the due season for favor (Psalm 102:13-15).

Favor takes you from shame to fame! God said, in Isaiah 61:7-8, that *"for your shame ye shall have **double**; and for confusion they shall rejoice in their portion: therefore in their land they shall possess the **double**: everlasting joy shall be unto them. For I the LORD* love judgment, I hate robbery for burnt offering; and I will direct their work in truth, and I will make an everlasting covenant with them."

When a person wants to know if they had truly found favor with another person, they seek an affirmation to their prayers. For example, in 2 Samuel 14:22, Joab "*…fell to the ground on his face, and bowed himself, and thanked the king: and Joab said, today thy servant knoweth that I have found **grace** in thy sight, my lord, O king, in that the king hath fulfilled the request of his servant.*"

Queen Esther also used answered prayer as proof of favor. She told her husband, King Ahasuerus, that "*if I have found favor in thy sight, O king, and if it please the king, let my life be given me at my petition, and my people at my request*" (Esther 7:9).

When you connect with His favor, there is an answer to prayers and an establishment of your works. In Psalm 90:17, the Psalmist says "*…let the beauty of the LORD our God be upon us: and establish thou the work of our hands upon us; yea, the work of our hands establish thou it.*"

BY THE GRACE OF GOD I AM WHO I AM!

Dr. Jonah Adukwu, an erstwhile colleague in medical school and now the pastor of Divine Harvest revival assembly, Lokoja Kogi state, accosted me in 1993, as we returned from an early morning prayer for the nation at the University of Nigeria Enugu Campus (UNEC) on what I wanted my legacy in UNEC to say.

After thinking for a while, and with my knowledge of Jonah as a man not given to frivolities and grandstanding, I spoke assertively and authoritatively on what I believed

God wanted my legacy to be. Borrowing from the words of Apostle Paul, in 1 Corinthians 15:10, I told him I want it to be said of me after UNEC that "...*by the grace of God I am what I am:....*"

He nodded, as a man of understanding that he is would, and walked away. Today, nearly 30 years later I can say "...*by the grace of God I am what I am: and his grace which was bestowed upon me was not in vain; but I labored more abundantly than they all: yet not I, but the grace of God which was with me*" (1 Corinthians 15:10).

Prayer: Encompass me with favor as with a shield, O Lord, in Jesus name!

PART II

Profiles in Gracing Favor

- David
- Samuel
- Ezra
- Mary
- Joseph
- Esther
- Noah
- Nehemiah
- Daniel
- Job
- Jesus

If you worked for everything you have, you won't live long enough to enjoy it!

—Archbishop Benson Idahosa
(1938-1998).

CHAPTER EIGHT

DAVID: A PROFILE IN GRACING FAVOR

*"...whom God drave out before the face of our fathers, unto the days of David; Who found **favor** before God, and desired to find a tabernacle for the God of Jacob"* (Acts 7:45-46).

Favor is permanent, powerful, and pillaging! The favor David prayed for from Achish, King of Gath, returned unto him in the form of a breakthrough beyond what he could imagine. He had asked for a little lot of a land, but got the town of Ziklag instead. He needed a slot for a solution, but instead got a permanent fortress on the map of Israel through favor.

In 1 Samuel 27:5-6, David prayed King Achish saying *"...if I have now found **grace** (or favor) in thine eyes, let them give me a place in some town in the country, that I may dwell there: for why should thy servant dwell in the royal city with thee? Then Achish gave him Ziklag that day:*

wherefore Ziklag pertaineth unto the kings of Judah unto this day."

Favor is generous, and goes beyond what is asked or requested. It is also rapid! Within twenty four hours, David and his men went from squatters to landlords. It was a significant turnaround, and happened notwithstanding disfavor from the top echelon of King Achish's Philistine army (see 1 Samuel 29:4-6).

Favor is not **fair**, or **frugal**, and need be only in the eyes of a **few** to take root. It took David having favor with ***God alone*** (Acts 7:46), to become a man after God's heart (Acts 13:22), the sweet Psalmist of Israel (2 Samuel 23:1), the most decorated General in their history (1 Chronicles 22:8), and the one whose progeny the King of Kings was raised (1 Chronicles 17:11-14).

DAVID VERSUS SAUL

The sweet Psalmist of Israel found favor with Saul, when the King of Israel – Saul - was living in disfavor before God. The story of King Saul, who was the first anointed king of Israel (1 Samuel 10:1), is one of the most tragic in the Bible. He died in ignominy and as one whose "...*shield of the mighty* (was) *vilely cast away,* (and whose)...*shield*...(was) *as though he had not been anointed with oil*" (2 Samuel 1:21).

He was slow to obey and gave up his glorious favor for a shameful death on the hills of Gilboa. In 1 Samuel 28:18, he was declared as one that "...*obeyedst not the voice of the LORD, nor executedst his fierce wrath upon Amalek, therefore hath the LORD done this thing unto thee this day."*

When God told him to "...*go and smite Amalek, and utterly destroy all that they have, and spare them not; but slay both man and woman, infant and suckling, ox and sheep, camel and ass*" (1 Samuel 15:3), he instead "...*spared the best of the sheep and of the oxen, to sacrifice unto the LORD thy God; and the rest...utterly destroyed*" (1 Samuel 15:15).

The aftermath of this was the loss of God's favor upon his life, and God picking David instead to lead Israel (see 1 Samuel 13:13-14). David, unlike Saul, was swift to respond to commands and fulfilled his obligations without equanimity and as a result he walked in unsurpassed favor.

In 1 Samuel 16:22-23, the Bible says "...*Saul sent to Jesse, saying, Let David, I pray thee, stand before me; for he hath found **favor** in my sight. And it came to pass, when the evil spirit from God was upon Saul, that David took an harp, and played with his hand: so Saul was refreshed, and was well, and the evil spirit departed from him.*"

David walked in sincerity and swiftness in carrying out King Saul's commands, and as a result the people loved him. The Bible says, in 1 Samuel 18:14-16, that "...*David behaved himself wisely in all his ways; and the LORD was with him. Wherefore when Saul saw that he behaved himself **very wisely**, he was afraid of him. But all Israel and Judah **loved David**, because he went out and came in before them.*"

His readiness to go and raid the Philistines and return victorious further endeared David to the people of Israel. He was described, in 1 Samuel 18:5, as *"David (who) went out whithersoever Saul sent him, and behaved himself wisely: and Saul set him over the men of war, and he was **accepted** in the sight of all the people, and also in the sight of Saul's servants."*

Those who go before men and serve God, without a lackadaisical attitude, but with sincerity and speed will return favored for their next level like David. He was not a hidden leader, with a hidden agenda in a hidden location but rather was open and transparent. As a result, the people loved him unabashedly and unashamedly and in the process irked King Saul when they sang "*…Saul hath slain his thousands, and David his ten thousands*" (1 Samuel 18:7).

Unlike King Saul who made rules he did not keep, and implemented things contrary to his own instructions (see 1 Samuel 28:9), David wore his heart on his sleeve and was transparent, truthful, and thoroughly professional in his activities. It was no wonder, therefore, that David waxed greater in favor (Acts 7:46) while King Saul drowned in dishonor and disfavor (2 Samuel 1:21).

DAVID AND JONATHAN

David and Jonathan made a covenant in 1 Samuel 18:3, which they renewed again in 1 Samuel 20:16-17. The latter scripture says, "*…Jonathan made a covenant with the house of David, saying, let the LORD even require it at the hand of David's enemies. And Jonathan caused David to swear **again**, because **he loved him**: for he loved him as **he loved his own soul**.*"

That love between them was the build up to the unprecedented gracing favor between both men and their families. They loved each other as their own soul, and it was that covenant of love and loyalty to one another that gave them and their progenitors **Gracing Favor**. Even after Jonathan died on mount Gilboa (1 Samuel 31:2), David kept this covenant and took Mephibosheth into his palace.

He asked, in 2 Samuel 9:1, "*Is there yet any that is left of the house of Saul, that I may shew him kindness for Jonathan's sake?*" After been informed of Mephibosheth, David said to Mephibosheth "*...I will surely shew thee kindness for Jonathan thy father's sake, and will restore thee all the land of Saul thy father; and thou shalt eat bread at my table continually*" (2 Samuel 13:7).

It was the love shed abroad in David's heart, and the favor it generated, that catapulted Mephibosheth and his family from the desolate town of Lodebar to the King's palace in Jerusalem. It was that same love that brought restoration (or grace) to Mephiboshet. Love is a critical factor in changing grass to grace and loathing to loving.

FOLURUNSHO ALAKIJA: FROM SUPREME STITCHES TO STATUS SYMBOL!

Mrs. Folurunsho Alakija is the Executive Vice Chairperson of FAMFA oil. She was born into a polygamous family, and while exposed to the life of business by her property-rich father and market goods sales mother, she began to imbibe a business that would serve her well in the future.

After attending a boarding school in Wales and Sagamu, Ogun State for high school, she returned to England to attend the American College, London and the Central School of Fashion, London for a degree in secretarial studies and fashion designing respectively.

On graduation, she returned to Nigeria and worked as the Private secretary to the chif executive officer First National Bank of Chicago, now First City Monument bank. She rose to become the head of the corporate affairs division, and left to pursue other interests she felt would allow her creative and business acumen blossom.

These interests included a fashion chain called *Supreme Stitches*, and an oil company called FAMFA oil. The latter metamorphosed at the request of some of her highbrow clients, who wanted to reward her for dressing them so elegantly. One of these was Mrs. Maryam Babangida, the famed wife of the then President, and through her executive reach and much prayer, Mrs. Alakija got an oil well, named Agbami OPL 216, allocated to her.

While in pursuit of the oil well, Mrs. Alakija had a spiritual awakening. She became born-again, and made a covenant with God to use whatever proceeds she generated from her oil business to glorify Him. She set up the Rose of Sharon foundation, to cater for widows, and even opened the Rose of Sharon Church as a platform for ministry.

Meanwhile, she had dragged the Nigerian government to court. After striking oil at the 617,000 acre offshore oil block, the government demanded a forfeiture of the whole oil block back to them. She resisted, and with the help of God, defeated the federal government at the Supreme court. She has since fully commercialized her OPL 216 oil well, and alongside her foundation, functions as the CEO at both organizations.

She has been recognized several times as the richest woman in the world, and is a frequent speaker at Churches, conferences, and cultural programs. She is happily married to her husband of forty five years, Modupe Alakija, and has two children who participate actively in the family business. Her life is a testament of ***Gracing Favor*** and resilience in life.

Prayer: I receive the power to get wealth, in Jesus name!

No Matter how many Birds fly in the Sky, they never collide with each other. So likewise must Christians fly without fear of competition or collison!

—Archbishop Benson Idahosa
(1938-1998)

CHAPTER NINE

SAMUEL: A PROFILE IN GRACING FAVOR

*"And the child Samuel grew on, and was in **favor** both with the LORD, and also with men"* (1 Samuel 2:26).

When Hannah entered into a covenant relationship with God, by dedicating her yet unborn son – Samuel - unto the Lord, it broke barrenness from her life and birth a spirit of favor that was carried by Samuel into ministry. In 1 Samuel 2:26, the Bible says *"…the child Samuel grew on, and was in favor both with the LORD, and also with men."*

From his vantage point of living in the temple, Samuel had a front row seat on how God's favor can turn a young boy's life into a prophetic battling ram for a nation, and how disfavor can eclipse years of priestly service as exhibited by the Eli family. He did not need any affirmation from the Eli family, but rather pursued God relentlessly and persistently.

Towards the end of his leadership of the nation, Samuel charged the people to "...*turn not aside from following the LORD, but **serve the LORD** with all your heart; And turn ye not aside: for then should ye go after vain things, which cannot profit nor deliver; for they are vain. For the LORD will not forsake his people for his great name's sake:* because it hath ***pleased the LORD*** to make you his people" (1 Samuel 12:20-22).

Even though the people of Israel had rejected Samuel and his son's leadership (1 Samuel 8:5), Samuel did not look at this sudden disfavor before men as the end. Rather, he maintained favor before God and in deference to this holy relationship with God, told the people "...*as for me, God forbid that I should sin against the LORD in ceasing to pray for you: but I will teach you the good and the right way*" (1 Samuel 12:23).

ELI VERSUS SAMUEL

Between Eli and Samuel, the former epitomizes disfavor (1 Samuel 4:21) while the latter epitomizes favor (1 Samuel 2:26). When the prophet spoke to Eli, about his being slow to rein in his children for their sins at the altar (see 1 Samuel 2:27-34), Eli offered no resistance or rebuttal.

The prophetic word from the Lord, according to the prophet, was that "...*them that honor me I will honor, and they that despise me shall be lightly esteemed* (or disfavored). *Behold, the days come, that I will cut off thine arm, and the arm of thy father's house, that there shall not be an old man in thine house and...the man of thine, whom I shall not cut off from mine altar, shall be to consume thine eyes, and to grieve thine heart: and all the increase of thine house shall die in the flower of their age"* (1 Samuel 2:30-33).

The tribe of Eli lived on as vestiges in Israel, till Doeg the Edomite decimated their lineage (in 1 Samuel 22:18-19) in fulfillment of this prophecy. They became outcasts, who were lampooned and alienated because their father was unwilling to do what God had continually told him. If he had obeyed, on the other hand, he would have seen glory, honor, and power in God's alter instead of shame and grief.

Samuel, on the other hand, went from a temple hand to being acknowledged as a trusted herald of God's word. In 1 Samuel 3:19-21, the Bible says "*...Samuel grew, and the LORD was with him, and did let none of his words fall to the ground. And all Israel from Dan even to Beersheba knew that Samuel was established to be a prophet of the LORD And the LORD* appeared again in Shiloh: for the LORD revealed himself to Samuel in Shiloh by the word of the LORD.*"*

THE ABSENCE OF PEACE IS PROOF OF THE ABSENCE OF GRACING FAVOR!

When Samuel was doing his salutary greetings to the children of Israel, he asked them if any of them could impugn his integrity. He said, "*...I have walked before you from my childhood unto this day. Behold, here I am: witness against me before the LORD, and before his anointed: whose ox have I taken? or whose ass have I taken? or whom have I defrauded? whom have I oppressed? or of whose hand have I received any bribe to blind mine eyes therewith? and I will restore it you. And they said, Thou hast not defrauded us,* *nor oppressed us, neither hast thou taken ought of any man's hand"* (1 Samuel 12:2-4).

They could not accuse him of any crime, or illegality, and he told them he had nothing against them and would keep praying for them nonetheless (1 Samuel 12:23). When the believer stops struggling with sin, and has peaceful relationships with God and man instead, he receives the anointing for Gracing Favor. In Romans 5:1, Apostle Paul says "...*being justified by faith, we have peace with God through our Lord Jesus Christ."*

When God pours out His grace, coupled with His mercy (or favor), your feet will not fail, and He (God) will deal bountifully with that individual. In Psalm 116:5-9, the Psalmist said "***gracious*** *is the* L<small>ORD</small>, *and righteous; yea, our God is merciful* (or **favoring)**... (and so)...*hast delivered my soul from death, mine eyes from tears, and my feet from falling*...(and) *I will walk before the* L<small>ORD</small> *in the land of the living."*

The will of God for you and I is to have un paralleled rest in our souls, and be delivered from premature death when we get Gracing favor. Most of all, however, He wants us to walk before His presence in the land of the living. He said, in Psalm 103:2-5, "*bless the* L<small>ORD</small>, *O my soul, and forget not all his benefits...who crowneth thee with* **lovingkindness** (Grace) *and tender* **mercies** (favor); *who satisfieth thy mouth with good things; so that thy youth is renewed like the eagle's."*

M<small>S</small>. B<small>URKE</small>: G<small>OD'S</small> I<small>RON</small> L<small>ADY</small>

Ms. Juanita Burke is a *mother in Israel* at the Assembly, West Monroe Louisiana (TAWM). She has lived over the last Ninety two years in perfect health and peace with God. She is a widow, whose husband was a clergyman in Oklahoma, and till date she takes no meds, and after a lifetime of sanctification still teaches Sunday School at TAWM.

She served as an English teacher at West Monroe High school for more than forty years, and was famed for enforcing English syntax that has shaped the lives of many of her students. She has edited several authors works (including *yours truly*), without charging any amount, and remains a passionate lover of God with focus on Bible inerrancy.

On one occasion, Ms. Burke went to bed and woke up to find a Toyota Camry in front of her house. Someone had dropped it off, and without been identified, had asked her to use it to God's glory and not sell it. That car has served her for more than 30 years, and enables her to do what God has called her to do. That is Gracing Favor!

Prayer: Revive thy glory and favor of God, in my life, O Lord in Jesus name!

Give God so much, you kill the devil with envy!

—Tobe Momah M.D.

CHAPTER TEN

EZRA: A PROFILE IN GRACING FAVOR

*"For we were bondmen; yet our God hath not forsaken us in our bondage, but hath extended **mercy** (or favor) unto us in the sight of the kings of Persia, to give us a reviving, to set up the house of our God, and to repair the desolations thereof, and to give us a wall in Judah and in Jerusalem"* (Ezra 9:9).

Ezra was a scribe in Babylon, who went from Babylon to Jerusalem, to help with the reconstruction of the temple. The Bible says, in Ezra 7:6, that *"this Ezra went up from Babylon; and he was a ready scribe in the law of Moses, which the LORD God of Israel had given: and **the king granted him all his request**, according to the hand of the LORD his God upon him."*

The hand of God upon Ezra represents spiritual power and direction. He was surrendered to the will of

God, and as long as Ezra obeyed Him, God "...*set* (His) *tabernacle among* (him):...(so that His) *soul shall not abhor* (him)..." (Leviticus 26:11).

If, on the contrary, Ezra disobeyed God disfavor would have followed him. In Leviticus 26:20, God says He will "...*break the pride of...power; and...make your heaven as iron, and your earth as brass: And your strength shall be spent in vain: for your land shall not yield her increase, neither shall the trees of the land yield their fruits*" if you disobey Him.

God's goal for you and I is to be an excellent reflection of His glory. In Galatians 2:20-21, Apostle Paul said *"I am crucified with Christ: nevertheless I live; yet not I, but Christ liveth in me: and the life which I now live in the flesh I live by the faith of the Son of God, who loved me, and gave himself for me. I do not frustrate the* **grace** *of God."*

THE SCENT OF SURRENDER

Too many want favor without the fear of God, or grace that is short of the glory of God. That is fool hardy, and atrocious to Gracing favor. In Numbers 24, Balaam described Israel in glowing terms, but the reason they glowed was because at that time they were surrendered to God's will. The minute they got enamored with the Moabitish women, in Numbers 25:1-3, their favor became fraught with failure.

In Numbers 24:5-8, Balaam said *"how goodly are thy tents, O Jacob, and thy tabernacles, O Israel! As the valleys are they spread forth, as gardens by the river's side, as the trees of lign aloes which the* LORD *hath planted, and as cedar trees beside the waters. He shall pour the water out of his buckets, and his seed shall be in many waters, and his king shall be higher than Agag, and his kingdom shall be exalted. God brought him forth out of Egypt; he hath as it were the strength of an unicorn: he shall eat up the nations his enemies, and shall break their bones, and pierce them* (with)...*his arrows."*

When Israelite "...*people began to commit whoredom with the daughters of Moab and they called the people unto the sacrifices of their gods and the people did eat, and bowed down to their gods and Israel joined himself unto Baalpeor... the anger of the* LORD *was kindled against Israel and the* LORD *said unto Moses, Take all the heads of the people, and hang them up before the* LORD *against the sun, that the fierce anger of the* LORD *may be turned away from Israel"* (Numbers 25:1-4).

Their erstwhile favor, that had made them un cursable by Balaam and impregnable to the Midianites, turned out to be temporary. They, instead, became a hotbed of failure as Zimri brought a Midianitish woman, Cozbi, into the presence of the praying Israelites. This caused "...*those that died in the plague* (to be) *twenty and four thousand*" (Numbers 25:9), and the after effects of the curse on Israel lived on for decades (see Joshua 22:17).

FAVOR REVIVES; GRACE RESTORES!

When the children of Israel were living in captivity, many of them married foreign wives and as a result corrupted their Holy Seed! It was a cause for concern for Ezra and he pled in prayer for mercy in Ezra 9:9. As a result, this mercy - otherwise called grace or favor - birthed revival or strength in Israel.

In Ezra 9:9, Ezra the priest said "...*we were bondmen; yet our God hath not forsaken us in our bondage, but hath extended mercy* (or favor) *unto us in the sight of the kings of Persia, to give us a **reviving**, to set up the house of our God, and to **repair** the desolations thereof, and to give us a wall in Judah and in Jerusalem.*"

It takes favor to birth revival and it takes grace to restore strength! In the case of the captive Israelites, Ezra knew it would take favor to turn them from captives to champions and as a result prayed for divine favor upon them (Ezra 9:9). Favor is God's limitless tool adjudged to bring revival, deliverance, and turnaround to the nations. You are called to be favored, and as the apple of God's eyes (Zechariah 2:8), He won't stop until you enter your destiny of ***Gracing Favor.***

GEORGE FOREMAN: GOD'S GRACE FASHIONISTA!

George Foreman is a former two time World heavyweight champion, and retired from boxing in 1977 when he gave his life to Jesus Christ. He started preaching on street corners, and became an ordained minister of the Church of Jesus Christ in Houston, Texas.

He returned to boxing in 1987, with the goal of raising funds for a youth center he had developed to keep youth off the street. He had won an Olympic Gold medal at the 1968 Munich Olympics, after being a youth plagued by mugging and imbecile behavior, and felt that if he could get youth into a sports arena, they would be able to channel their energy in a more useful direction.

Amazingly, at 45 he won his second world heavyweight championship and after he retired in 1994 he was introduced to a company selling grills by his lawyer. He was given a couple to sample, and after his wife – Joan - told him how well they worked, he decided to be the face of the company.

Within five years, the company had sold millions of the famed Foreman grill with George getting 40% of the profit on each grill. Spectrum industries, the makers of the George Foreman grill, then decided to buy out George's name with a sum of $125 million and together with the estimated $4 million he had earned per month while using his name it is estimated George garnered more than $300 million from the George Foreman grill.

He states that notwithstanding his success in commerce and sports, his greatest achievement is knowing Jesus as Lord and savior. A father of eleven children, George credits God for delivering him from the pressures of his youth and a near death experience after a fight in Peurto-Rico. At seventy three years of age, he still runs the George Foreman youth center and is a regular speaker at Churches and men's conferences.

Prayer: May the anointing of Gracing Favor open doors to limitless wealth and power, in Jesus name.

One Day of Favor is Greater than a Lifetime of Labor!

—Matthew Ashimolowo
Senior Pastor, Kingsway International
Christian Center, London UK

CHAPTER ELEVEN

MARY: A PROFILE IN GRACING FAVOR

> *"And the angel said unto her, Fear not, Mary: for thou hast found **favor** with God. And, behold, thou shalt conceive in thy womb, and bring forth a son, and shalt call his name JESUS."* (Luke 1:30-31).

Faith, otherwise called strength in Romans 4:17, is the reason Mary outshone her peers in favor. Mary's response to the Angel's statement, at 13 years, that she would *"...conceive in thy womb, and bring forth a son,* (as)... *the Holy Ghost shall come upon* (her)..., *and the power of the Highest shall overshadow* (her)" (Luke 1:28-35) was full of faith and not doubt.

She said, in Luke 1:38, *"...behold the handmaid of the Lord; be it unto me according to thy word. And the angel departed from her."* A similar scenario had earlier played out with high priest Zechariah, but unlike Mary, he was made dumb after the Angel noted unbelief in his answer (see Luke 1:20).

Mary, even though she found the Angel's message hard to understand, responded with a heart full of faith and belief. She was attested by Elizabeth, as "…(one) *that believed: for there shall be a performance of those things which were told her from the Lord*" (Luke 1:45). No wonder she was the only person acknowledged in scripture as *highly favored* (Luke 1:28).

FAVOR: FUEL FOR THE FUTURE!

The earthly womb that bare Jesus needed favor to conceive! Mary bore Jesus in her womb for nine months, but before that she was heralded by the angel, in Luke 1:26-35, as "…*highly favored,* (for) *the Lord is with thee* (and) *blessed art thou among women.*"

The effect of this favor was the manifestation of Jesus without a male and female concupiscence. **Favor is the root ground for the miraculous.**

The high favor Mary was heralded with was the result of her stellar service in the kingdom of God. She described herself, in Luke 1:38 in this regard. She said "…*behold the handmaid of the Lord; be it unto me according to thy word.*" In Luke 1:48, she added that God "…*hath regarded the low estate of his handmaiden: for, behold, from henceforth all generations shall call me blessed.*"

The word *handmaiden* is the Greek word *Doulos*, and it is interpreted as slave or bond person. The path to high favor is paved with service. No wonder this same Mary was called by the angel to "…*fear not, Mary: for thou hast found favor with God*" (Luke 1:30).

FAVOR AS A WEAPON!

The number one weapon we have against shame is Favor. The favor of God is the cause for the obliteration of shame. When Mary was found to be with child, and was about to be ashamed and assaulted, the angel appeared to Joseph and told him "...*Joseph, thou son of David, fear not to take unto thee Mary thy wife: for that which is conceived in her is of the Holy Ghost. And she shall bring forth a son, and thou shalt call his name JESUS: for he shall save his people from their sins*" (Matthew 1:20-21).

Favor stops shame in its tracks! The mindset of shame needs to be replaced with a love for favor. The wise man said "*a good name is rather to be chosen than great riches, and **loving favor** rather than silver and gold*" (Proverbs 22:1). Too many people live in shame, rather than love favor and as a result they paralyze their future.

If Mary had lived ashamed, and not accepted God's favor, she would never have become the birth mother of Jesus. It takes acceptance by God to gain approval by men. In Romans 14:17-18, Apostle Paul says, "*...the kingdom of God is not meat and drink; but righteousness, and peace, and joy in the Holy Ghost. For he that in these things serveth Christ is **acceptable to God, and approved of men.**"*

Favor is your ticket to divine acceptance and stops human rejection immediately. Even though she went against the climes and culture of her day, she refused to be ashamed or distance herself from her "unclaimed" pregnancy with Jesus. She was time and time again at Jesus meetings, and remained stable in her conviction of Him as the Son of God to the end.

PRISED AWAY BY A CRIMINAL, BUT PRAISED BACK BY CHRIST!

Willie Myrick, a Nine year old Atlanta teen, was walking in front of his South Atlanta home when he was lured away by a young man into his car with the promise of money. He was thrown in the bonnet of the car, and driven around Atlanta for three hours.

While locked up in the bonnet of the car, Willie began to sing words to the famous song ***Every Praise belongs to our God*** by Hezekiah Walker. His captor cursed at him repeatedly, and commanded him to stop. Willie, however, continued to sing for three hours straight.

According to Willie, he had been taught in Sunday School at Mount Carmel Baptist Church, Atlanta that if you praised God he would do mysterious things to rescue you. He, therefore, persisted in his praise much to the chagrin of his captors. Eventually, his captor dropped him off at the East point area of Atlanta and asked him to tell no one.

Instead, Willie is telling everyone! After been dropped off, he called his mother from an elderly woman's phone and credits his Godmother for taking him to Church and teaching him the Bible. He states that his favorite scripture is Psalm 23, and even though threatened, cursed and ordered not to reveal the identity by his captor, Willie drew a picture that eventually led Police to arrest the captor. Truly, The Lord is Willie's Shepherd!

Prayer: Baptize me with the spirit of unalloyed service to you, O Lord, in Jesus name!

Your Glory does not Depend on your Labor, but on God's Favor!

—Tobe Momah M.D.

CHAPTER TWELVE

JOSEPH: A PROFILE IN GRACING FAVOR

*"And the patriarchs, moved with envy, sold Joseph into Egypt: but God was with him, and delivered him out of all his afflictions, and gave him **favor** and wisdom in the sight of Pharaoh king of Egypt; and he made him governor over Egypt and all his house"* (Acts 7:9-10).

While Joseph was in the pit (Genesis 37:24), house of Potiphar (Genesis 39:2), or the Egyptian prison (Genesis 39:20-21), he had one common denominator called **Grace** and **Favor** working for him. He rose up the ladder of Egyptian society, not based on his educational acumen, religious affiliation, royal pedigree, or military prowess but on the basis of God's grace and favor.

In Genesis 39:2-6, the Bible says "...*the* L*ord* was with Joseph, and he was a prosperous man; and he was in the house of his master the Egyptian. And his master saw that the LORD was with him, and that the LORD made all that he did to prosper in his hand. And Joseph found **grace** *in his sight, and he served him: and he made him overseer over his house, and all that he had he put into his hand* (for)*…Joseph was a goodly person, and **well favored**.*"

The secret to these unprecedented achievements by a slave in a foreign land was *gracing favor*. Rather than align himself with the idols of Egypt, Joseph situated himself with the Lord God Almighty (see Genesis 39:21). As a result, God "*…delivered him out of all his afflictions, and gave him favor and wisdom in the sight of Pharaoh king of Egypt; and he made him governor over Egypt*" (Acts 7:10).

JOSEPH: THE APOSTLE OF FAVOR

Joseph was in prison, and yet ascended to the throne of Egypt as Prime Minister. In Genesis 39:21, the Bible says *"the LORD was with Joseph, and shewed him mercy, and gave him **favor** in the sight of the keeper of the prison. And the keeper of the prison committed to Joseph's hand all the prisoners that were in the prison; and whatsoever they did there, he was the doer of it…because the LORD was with him, and that which he did, the LORD made it to prosper.*"

Even through some of the most unfortunate circumstances in Joseph's life, *gracing favor* showed up. In Genesis 39:4-5, "*…Joseph found **grace** in his* (Potiphar) *sight, and he served him: and he made him overseer over his house, and all that he had he put into his hand. And it came to pass from the time that he had made him overseer in his house, and over all that he had, that the LORD blessed the Egyptian's house for Joseph's sake;….*"

His time in jail is described further in Psalm 105:17-22. It says God "*...sent a man before them, even Joseph, who was sold for a servant: Whose feet they hurt with fetters: he was laid in iron: Until the time that his word came: the word of the LORD tried him. The king sent and loosed him; even the ruler of the people, and let him go free. He made him lord of his house, and ruler of all his substance: To bind his princes at his pleasure; and teach his senators wisdom.*"

The Church are called to favor, not shame! That is why Jospeh later on tells his brothers to "*...tell my father of my glory in Egypt...*" (Genesis 45:13). **The architect of his glory was his favor with God and man.** He was a future predecessor of the suffering Christ and through his actions, changed the trajectory of the Egyptian nation. He took them from shame to fame, from poverty to prosperity, from scanty to surplus, and from dream to destiny.

FAVOR IS A GAME CHANGER OVER SHAME!

Without a heart set on service, Joseph may never have seen the favor of the Lord. He could have gone to Potiphar's house, the prison, or the palace and focused on his woe alone but instead in each of these places he set out to serve. He was described, in Psalm 105:17-22, as "*...the ruler of the people, ...lord of his house, and ruler of all his substance to bind his princes at his pleasure; and teach his senators wisdom.*"

The aftermath of this was unrivalled favor. In Genesis 39:2-4, the Bible says "*...the LORD was with Joseph, and he was a prosperous man; and he was in the house of his master the Egyptian. And his master saw that the LORD* was with him, and that the L*ORD* made all that he did to prosper in his hand. And Joseph found **grace** *in his sight, and he served him: and he made him overseer over his house, and all that he had he put into his hand."*

After that period of service, "*...it came to pass from the time that he had made him overseer in his house, and over all that he had, that the L*ORD* blessed the Egyptian›s house for Joseph›s sake; and the blessing of the L*ORD* was upon all that he had in the house, and in the field. And he left all that he had in Joseph›s hand; and he knew not ought he had, save the bread which he did eat. And Joseph was a **goodly** person, and **well favored**"* (Genesis 39:5-6).

Without favor, Joseph would have been lost in the obscurity of Egypt but his life of surrender stimulated the oil of favor that brought him before Pharaoh. The Bible describes him in glowing terms at the benedictory blessings of Jacob. The patriarch blessed him saying, "*Joseph is a fruitful bough, even a fruitful bough by a well; whose branches run over the wall: The archers have sorely grieved him, and shot at him, and hated him: But his bow abode in strength, and the arms of his hands were made strong by the hands of the mighty God of Jacob..."* (Genesis 49:22-24).

Though estranged from the rest of his siblings, and vilified by so-called friends and associates, Joseph's surrender to God never wavered. This un paralleled strength in God (Genesis 49:24) resulted in unprecedented good will, and resulted in him having unparalleled favor that made him first among equals in Egypt (Genesis 41:44). No wonder the Psalmist said *"all the paths of the L*ORD* are **mercy** and **truth** unto such as keep his covenant and his testimonies"* (Psalm 25:10).

BENSON IDAHOSA, AND THE ORACLE OF ILESHA.

When Pa Elton, an American Missionary based in Ilesha, Oyo Nigeria met with Idahosa he prayed a prayer of limitless resources upon him. He (Archbishop Idahosa) then had a vision of a blood washed Africa and soon after instituted a Church in Benin called Church of God Mission (CGM) international with the motto *Evangelism is our supreme task*.

He organized a successful crusade in Benin city, and wanted to replicate it through out Nigeria. He was enthusiastic, as was his then 200 member Church, but short of finances. He had what he (Idahosa) fondly called *anointing without abundance that births annoyance*.

He began to travel the world, preaching the uncompromised Word of God and on one of his travels, God gave instruction to Gordon Lindsay - while on a retreat in Israel - to sponsor Idahosa's studies abroad. He spoke to him and told him to give the then Rev. Idahosa enough funds to fund his training in America, alongside free books, transport, tuition, and any upkeep allowance he needed.

Though they had never met, Gordon Lindsay requited the funds to Idahosa through Pa Elton and it afforded him a seamless two year education at the Christ for the Nations Bible Institute (CFNI), in Dallas, Texas, USA.

On return from Dallas, and buoyed by his recent international exposure, he launched into a television ministry that made him a household name in Nigeria. He preached to more white and black men than any other black man alive or dead, and took the gospel to more than 138 countries.

At its peak, CGM was roofing one Church building a week and opening a new Church branch daily. By the time of his death in 1998, he had planted more than six thousand CGM Churches, and opened a vista of communication with America's elite preachers including Oral Roberts, T.L Osborne, Kenneth Hagin, and Kenneth Copeland.

Prayer: Make me stand favored before kings and men, O Lord, in Jesus name.

The Favor of God Requires High, Handy, and Holy Maintenance

—Tobe Momah M.D.

CHAPTER THIRTEEN

ESTHER: A PROFILE IN GRACING FAVOR

> *"...Esther obtained **favor** in the sight of all them that looked upon her. So Esther was taken unto king Ahasuerus into his house royal in the tenth month, which is the month Tebeth, in the seventh year of his reign. And the king loved Esther above all the women, and she obtained **grace** and **favor in** his sight more than all the virgins; so that he set the royal crown upon her head, and made her queen instead of Vashti"* (Esther 2:15-17).

There are people who experienced ***Gracing favor*** and their lives were unparalleled as a result. Esther was such an example. An orphan, who was raised by her uncle, she rose to become the Queen of an empire that spanned 127 provinces from Asia to India. At the height of her success, she uncovered a plot by Haman, the prime Minister, to annihilate her and her people.

In the defense of her people to her husband, King Ahasuerus, she said "...*if I have found **favor** in thy sight, O king, and if it please the king, let my life be given me at my petition, and my people at my request. For we are sold, I and my people, to be destroyed, to be slain, and to perish. But if we had been sold for bondmen and bondwomen, I had held my tongue, although the enemy could not countervail the king's damage*"(Esther 7:3-4).

Favor was the platform upon which the rescue of a whole nation was based! No matter the opposition one may face, favor is always a game changer! In Psalm 30:5-7, the Psalmist said "...*His anger endureth but a moment; **in his favor is life**: weeping may endure for a night, but joy cometh in the morning. And in my prosperity I said, I shall never be moved. LORD, by **thy favor** thou hast made my mountain to stand strong:....*"

Esther was faced with an impossible situation, but her faith stood strong because of favor! She told her uncle Mordecai, in Esther 4:16, that "...*I go in unto the king, which is not according to the law: and if I perish, I perish.*"She broke protocol to save a people, and crossed boundaries to build a heritage, and suceeded through favor.

When she stood before the King eventually, on day three of her fast, "...*she obtained **favor** in his sight: and the king held out to Esther the golden sceptre that was in his hand...saying...what wilt thou, queen Esther? and what is thy request? it shall be even given thee to the half of the kingdom*" (Esther 5:2-3). That is the Power of **Gracing Favor!**

Prayer: An instrument for Favor

Favor is for the faithful in the place of prayer. It followed Esther as she stood in the presence of the King, after three days of prayer and fasting (Esther 4:16). It helped her and her nation overcome the wicked machinations of Haman and his cohorts, and turned the tide of evil against their adversaries.

In Esther 8:11, after been petitioned by Queen Esther, the "...*king granted the Jews which were in every city to gather themselves together, and to stand for their life, to destroy, to slay and to cause to perish, all the power of the people and province that would assault them, both little ones and women, and to take the spoil of them for a prey.*"

Instead of victims, they became victors and instead of being annihilated, they got advanced! The platform of favor resisted the weapons of the enemy, without lifting a sword in its own defense. Esther and Mordecai favored God's righteous cause and He, in turn, fought their enemies to a standstill!

In Psalm 37:26-27, the Psalmist said "...*let them be ashamed and brought to confusion together that rejoice at mine hurt: let them be clothed with shame and dishonor that magnify themselves against me. Let them shout for joy, and be glad, that **favor my righteous cause:** yea, let them say continually, Let the* Lord *be magnified, which hath pleasure in the prosperity of his servant.*"

Favor for the Impossible

Favor, otherwise called grace, kindness, or mercy, is the reason Esther outshone her peers in favor. When pitched against the prettiest girls in the empire, Esther may not have had jaw dropping dead-gorgeous looks like some of them did, but she had a spirit of grace and favor that outcast and outlasted them.

In Esther 2:11, she "...*pleased him* (Hegai), *and... obtained **kindness** (favor) of him; and he speedily gave her her things for purification, with such things as belonged to her, and seven maidens, which were meet to be given her, out of the king's house: and he **preferred** her and her maids unto the best place of the house of the women.*"

Being raised without a tutelage in etiquette, nor in an environment steeped with protocol, Esther was the most unlikely to succeed in the King's palace. She was, however, so covered in favor and grace that she "... *obtained **favor** in the sight of all them that looked upon her*" (Esther 2:15).

Notwithstanding the uphill task she faced, Esther rose to the challenge. She believed the words of her Uncle (Esther 2:10), and God gave her favor that was uncommon and near impossible. After her one night with the King, "...*the king loved Esther above all the women, and she obtained **grace** and **favor** in his sight more than all the virgins; so that he set the royal crown upon her head, and made her queen instead of Vashti*" (Esther 2:15).

Without following Mordecai's instructions, favor for the impossible would not have been possible! Who you follow truly determines what follows you, and who you see will determine who sees you! Esther was faithful to her Uncle Mordecai, as showcased in her determination not to acquiesce as a Queen to Haman's holocaust, but go high strung to save her people (Esther 5:1-8). As a result, she birthed a *gracing favor* that gave the "... *Jews...light, and gladness, and joy, and honor*" (Esther 8:16).

THE TRIALS, TRAVAILS AND TRIUMPH OF CHRISTINE CAINE

The founder of *A21* and *Propel Woman*, Christine Caine, was taken from an orphanage at one month of age and adopted by her parents. Her adoptive parents were Greek Migrants to Australia and she re-collects at different forua the stigma and ostracization she faced growing up in a culture which considered her a second-class citizen.

As a result of her past, she was made fun of and called several derogatory words. She was abused from the age of four till she was Sixteen Years old by four different men sexually and psychologically. She was placed on government funding, lived in the projects, and subsumed by an environment that institutionalized mediocrity and poverty.

On one occasion, she went to the guidance counsellor in her High School and told her she wanted to undergo a University education in Australia. The counsellor told her she was from the wrong side of the divide, and had no hope of achieving her dreams.

She later became a Christian, and after joining Hill song Church at 22 years, got to understand who she was in Christ and pursued attending College intentionally.

She eventually graduated with a degree in English and economic development.

She met her husband, Nick, at College and at the age of thirty she got married to him. At the turn of her thirty third year of life, an even greater awakening about who she was in Christ came upon her. Her brother, got a letter from the Government of Australia telling him he had been adopted by his parents. As he went to confront his mother with the letter, Christine followed him.

As her brother confronted their mother, Christine was told pointblank by her mother that she too had been adopted. She was shown a paper from the department of health that stated that she was unwanted by her biological mother.

Rather than retreating into her shell in shame, Christine opened her mouth and said God "*…hast covered me in my* (original) *mother's womb…for I am fearfully and wonderfully made: marvelous are* (His) *works; and that my soul knoweth right well. My substance was not hid from* (Him), *when I was made in secret, and curiously wrought in the lowest parts of the earth.* (His) *eyes did see my substance, yet being unperfect; and in* (His) *book all my members were written…*" (Psalm 139:13-16).

Since that eventual day, Christine Caine has risen from being a youth leader at Hillsong Church, Australia to being a global voice for the voiceless all around the world. She leads, as the founder of *A21*, a mission dedicated to eradicating slavery in the world and organizes *Propel Woman* conferences around the world. She is also a reputed key note speaker at various Church and women conferences.

She has written six books, including *unstoppable* and *unashamed*, that have gone on to become best sellers and today is living a life – alongside her Pastor Husband and daughters - that has eclipsed her once embarrassing existence. Their ministry encompasses the *Zoe* Churches, located mostly in the Eastern Europe area, and these Churches have carved a niche for themselves by giving a voice to marginalized and disenfranchised locales.

Prayer: Baptize my life with double honor and triple favor, in Jesus name, O Lord.

__Many Christians only know opportunity; they don't know importunity!__
__...Bishop Emmah Gospel Isong__

(Christian Central Chapel Calabar, Nigeria)

CHAPTER FOURTEEN

NOAH: A PROFILE IN GRACING FAVOR

> *"And the* LORD *said, I will destroy man whom I have created from the face of the earth; both man, and beast, and the creeping thing, and the fowls of the air; for it repenteth me that I have made them. But Noah found **grace** in the eyes of the* LORD*"* (GENESIS 6:7-8).

When all the world was about to be destroyed, one man found *gracing favor* that spared he, and his family from destruction. In Genesis 6:8, the Bible teaches about this innate power of Gracing Favor. It shows how *gracing favor* marks one out for deliverance, preservation, and distinction (1 Peter 3:20).

In Genesis 6:8-9, the Bible teaches that amidst a worldwide armageddon, *"Noah found **grace** in the eyes of the* LORD*…(and) Noah was a just man and perfect in his* *generations, and Noah walked with God."* The word used for **Grace** in Genesis 6:8 is the Hebrew word ***Chenan,*** and it means gracious, favored, kindness, and pleasant.

As we get to the close of the age, and a repetition of the days of Noah are imminent (Matthew 24:37 and Luke 17:26-27), so must the same *gracing favor*, righteousness, and justness that kept Noah preserved become common place in the Church. The apostle Peter says, God *"… spared not the old world, but **saved Noah** the eighth person, a preacher of righteousness, bringing in the flood upon the world of the ungodly"* (2 Peter 2:5).

Just like *gracing favor* kept Noah and his family, so will it preserve the last day Church. Despite the world being on the precipice currently, a remnant will be spared. These remnant are those who walk in God's grace and favor, and as it *"…was in the days of Noe, so shall it be also in the days of the Son of man"* (Luke 17:26).

THE FEW, THE FAVORED AND THE FEARED

Noah was a minority of minorities over the one hundred years he preached righteousness to the people of his day (Genesis 5:32 and 7:6). Rather than respond in faith, they jettisoned Noah's words and ended up destroyed. It does not take a majority to sway God's opinion, as eventually only Noah, his wife, their three sons and wives were saved (1 Peter 3:20 and 2 Peter 2:5).

On opening the Ark, Noah made an offering from the few animals available, and gave it to God as a burnt offering (Genesis 8:20). In response, *"God smelled a sweet savor; and the LORD said in his heart, I will not again curse the ground any more for man's sake...* (for) *while the earth remaineth, seedtime and harvest, and cold and heat, and summer and winter, and day and night shall not cease"* (Genesis 8:21-22).

Noah gave a precious seed, and God gave him and the generations following a precious promise! It is the preciousness of the seed that determines the posterity of its action. That seed Noah sowed, in the aftermath of the flood, stopped future floods and invoked the lifetime law of seedtime and harvest (Genesis 8:22).

This law captures the essence of Gracing Favor, but it was the product of a sacrificial seed. The astounding favor God showed Noah was from a lifetime of faithfulness lived in the fear of the Lord. In Hebrews 11:7, the Bible says *"by faith Noah, being warned of God of things not seen as yet,* **moved with fear***, prepared an ark to the saving of his house; by the which he condemned the world, and became heir of the righteousness which is* **by faith***."*

RESIST, REPEAT, AND RECEIVE!

Noah obtained Gracing Favor from God through surrender. He is mentioned in Hebrews 11:7 as one of the patriarchs of the faith, and one whose lifestyle was a sharp contradiction to the unbridled corruption that was rife in his day.

In Genesis 6:5-9, the Bible says *"...God saw that the wickedness of man was great in the earth, and that every imagination of the thoughts of his heart was only evil continually. And it repented the* LORD *that he had made man on the earth, and it grieved him at his heart. And the* LORD *said, I will destroy man whom I have created from the face of the earth; both man, and beast, and the creeping thing, and the fowls of the air; for it repenteth me that I have made them."*

Notwithstanding the populist opinions of his day, or any extraneous erratum that going against the grain might result in, Noah jumped ship and did what was contrary to everything everyone considered normal in His time. In Luke 17:26-27, Jesus said "*…as it was in the days of Noe, so shall it be also in the days of the Son of man* (for) *they did eat, they drank, they married wives, they were given in marriage, until the day that Noah entered into the ark, and the flood came, and destroyed them all."*

Just like Noah needed favor, through the fear of the Lord and a surrendered life, to overcome the evil days he lived in so will believers require surrender that births favor if they want to thrive in these last days. Until you resist sin, you can't repeat the heroics of the saints, and receive the laurels they once were bestowed.

How Idahosa built Dangote!

Dr T.L and Daisy Osborne had spent an eventful week in Benin, Nigeria with Archbishop Benson Idahosa and his wife. They had ministered to thousands of ministers, preached to millions, and given away Peugeot station wagons and Bible literature to visiting pastors. They were fulfilled but needed to get on the next plane to Lagos if they were to catch their flight to Europe and then to the U.S.A for another urgent ministry assignment.

After preaching at the Faith Arena, Benin city Nigeria they drove with the Arch bishop to the airport. They had no seats for a flight from Benin, and were apprehensive about how he hoped to get them to Lagos that afternoon. They were supposed to leave Lagos for Europe, and their hopes were looking more and more forlorn but the Archbishop re-assured them and asked them to trust him.

On arrival, Archbishop Idahosa took his guests to the foot of the already fully-boarded plane which was readying for take off. He used his burly physique and intimidating posture to get the Pilot to stop take off and let he and his guests on the flight. As a well-known statesman in Nigeria generally, and Benin, in particular, he felt he could sway two of the passengers to give up their seats for his guests.

As he climbed the stairway, and acknowledged greetings from everyone around him, he proceeded to talk to the crew and passengers of this fully boarded and filled flight. He craved their attention, and indulgence, and explained who the Osbornes were and why they needed to be on that flight. He asked for two people to give up their seats and watch what God would do for them in response.

Everyone looked down, and nobody moved except two young men in the back. These men were business men, who were visiting Benin to explore business opportunities, and as they reluctantly stood up the Archbishop began to bless them. He said, "*as you stood up for my guests so will the world stand up for you.*" Those men were Aliko Dangote and his personal assistant.

Today, the world is truly standing up for Aliko Dangote and his man. He (Aliko Dangote) is worth nearly thirty Billion dollars, and for the last twenty years has been acknowledged as the richest person in Africa, and the wealthiest black person alive. He has seventy one subsidiaries, owns 26 companies, is listed on the world's biggest stock exchanges, and is building the one of the world's largest refineries in Lagos, Nigeria.

Prayer: Make my life an evidence of your Gracing favor, in Jesus name!

Every man's fear is his mountain and every man's mountain is his fear!

—Tobe Momah M.D.

CHAPTER FIFTEEN

NEHEMIAH: A PROFILE IN GRACING FAVOR

> *"O LORD, I beseech thee, let now thine ear be attentive to the prayer of thy servant, and to the prayer of thy servants, who desire to fear thy name: and prosper, I pray thee, thy servant this day, and grant him **mercy** (favor) in the sight of this man. For I was the king's cupbearer"* (Nehemiah 1:11).

Nehemiah was a major beneficiary of divine favor. He was the King's cupbearer, and under the burden of the tales of woe from Jerusalem, he expressed his grief in the King's presence (Nehemiah 2:1-2). This was unacceptable for the King's cupbearer, as according to Esther 4:2, *"… none might enter into the king's gate clothed with sackcloth."*

He had, however, prayed for ***Gracing Favor*** before he stepped into the King's presence. In Nehemiah 1:11, Nehemiah prayed saying *"O LORD, I beseech thee, let now* *thine ear be attentive to the prayer of thy servant, and to the prayer of thy servants, who desire to fear thy name: and prosper, I pray thee, thy servant this day, and grant him* **mercy** *(or favor) in the sight of this man...."*

The word mercy is from the same Greek root word – *Charis* – as favor! It (favor) means excess mercy, and grace is defined as divine ability. It was as a result of grace and favor that "...*the king granted* (Nehemiah), *according to the good hand of* (his)...*God upon*...(him)" (Nehemiah 2:8).

With the **Gracing Favor** of God upon him, therefore, it came as no surprise to onlookers when Nehemiah finished the walls of Jerusalem in Fifty two days. In Nehemiah 6:15-6, the Bible says "...*the wall was finished in the twenty and fifth day of the month Elul, in fifty and two days and it came to pass, that when all our enemies heard thereof, and all the heathen that were about us saw these things, they were much cast down in their own eyes: for they perceived that this work was wrought of our God.*"

WHEN GRACE AND FAVOR COLLIDE IN PRAYER!

It is not the works of man that produce the favor of God. Rather, the works of man can short circuit divine favor if they are not pre-empted by the Spirit of God. In Jeremiah 17:5-6, the Bible says, "...*cursed be the man that trusteth in man, and maketh flesh his arm, and whose heart departeth from the* LORD.... *he shall be like the heath in the desert, and shall not see when good cometh; but shall inhabit the parched places in the wilderness, in a salt land and not inhabited.*"

It took prayer, not the arm of flesh, for Nehemiah to connect with divine favor! In Nehemiah 2:4-6, the

Bible says "...*the king said unto me,...what dost thou make request? So I **prayed** to the God of heaven. And I said unto the king, If it please the king, and if thy servant have found favor in thy sight, that thou wouldest send me unto Judah, unto the city of my fathers' sepulchres, that I may build it. And the king said unto me, (the queen also sitting by him,)...how long shall thy journey be? and when wilt thou return? So it **pleased** the king to send me; and I set him a time.*"

There are few forces as potent as Grace and Favor when combined in prayer. In Nehemiah's case, "*...the king granted him, according to the good hand of my God upon* (him)" (Nehemiah 2:8). It (Gracing favor) unleashes an invincible force in the realm of prayer that no mortal or immortal force can withstand.

In Zechariah 12:9-10, the Bible says "*...it shall come to pass in that day, that I will seek to destroy all the nations that come against Jerusalem. And I will pour upon the house of David, and upon the inhabitants of Jerusalem, the spirit of grace and of supplications:....*"

There is a spirit of grace and supplications that destroys all the nations that come against the Church when evoked. The word *supplications* is the Hebrew word *tachanun*, and it means to entreat or seek favor. Nehemiah combined the grace of God's hand upon him and supplications that gave him favor to miraculously finish a long drawn out project in fifty two days, and shut the mouth of Israel's naysayers.

FROM DISGRACE TO GRACE BY FAVOR!

Nehemiah finished the walls of Jerusalem in fifty two days (Nehemiah 6:15) and saved the nation of Israel from disgrace (Nehemiah 1:3). The secret to this newfound favor Israel was shown, however, was supernatural strength! In Nehemiah 2:17, Nehemiah told the people of Jerusalem "...*see the distress that we are in, how Jerusalem lieth waste, and the gates thereof are burned with fire: come, and let us build up the wall of Jerusalem, that we be no more a reproach.*"

The strengthening of their hands, and their dependence on God for strength, brought out fresh favor that steeped Nehemiah in provision and protection. They responded with a commitment to depending on God for strength. They said, "*...let us rise up and build. So they **strengthened** their hands for this good work*" (Nehemiah 2:18).

Towards the end of the building campaign, and as they rebuilt the fallen walls of Jerusalem, Nehemiah prayed "*...now therefore, O God, strengthen my hands*" (Nehemiah 6:9). Strength is a function of favor; in Psalm 30:6-7, the Psalmist said "*...LORD, by thy favor thou hast made my mountain to stand strong:....*"

In other words, prayer, strength and favor rolled away the disgrace of Israel, and ushered in an era of grace. Without favor, however, strength would not have been available and without strength disgrace would have continued unabated. The establishment of our works, therefore, is the objective of Gracing Favor.

In Psalm 90:14-17, the Psalmist prayed "*...satisfy us early with thy **mercy**; that we may rejoice and be glad all our days. Make us glad according to the days wherein thou hast afflicted us, and the years wherein we have seen evil. Let thy work appear unto thy servants, and thy glory unto their* *children. And let the beauty of the LORD our God be upon us: and establish thou the work of our hands upon us;…"*

GENERAL. ONOJA ON GENERAL. MOMAH

The Godwin Orkar coup had just taken place in Nigeria. It was 1989, and a putsch of officers of Ibo extraction was taking place in the Nigerian army because many of those who betrayed the trust of the president, and broached access to the armory in Dodan Barracks, were Ibos.

The man compiling this list of *saboteurs* was the Army secretary and a contemporary of my father, General Sam Momah. Hs name was General Lawrence Onoja, and he went about his job with astuteness, and diligence. An Idoma, from Benue state, he and my late father had crossed paths during my late father's tour of duty in Benue state.

After a few months turned into a few years, and no list with my father's name was forthcoming, Sam bumped into General Onoja (who by now had become the Principal staff officer to General Abacha), and after some small talk, General Onoja looked at him matter of factly and told him something that shook my father to his foundations.

He said, as Army secretary, his name had risen for retirement on several occasions but on every occasion it was eventually removed. He then told my Dad, *whoever you are praying to, keep praying to Him because he definitely answers prayers*.

My Dad went on to become one of the few and only officers of his time to attain the rank of Major General in the Nigerian Army. He, also, served as the Minister of Science and Technology under two different military regimes, and a member of the highest ruling organ of government.

If he had been laid off in 1989, as planned by his enemies, he would not have achieved those laurels and seen those milestones. He prayed and fasted several times, to my knowledge, for promotion and favor with his superiors and God answered him with Gracing Favor. Halleluyah!

Prayer: Baptize me with a strength from above that gives me un common and high favor!

Don't carry gates, as a monument, but instead walk majestically through them!

—Tobe Momah M.D.

CHAPTER SIXTEEN

DANIEL: A PROFILE IN GRACING FAVOR

*"...king spake unto Ashpenaz the master of his eunuchs, that he should bring certain of the children of Israel, and of the king's seed, and of the princes; Children in whom was no blemish, but **well favored**, and skillful in all wisdom, and cunning in knowledge, and understanding science, and such as had ability in them to stand in the king's palace, and whom they might teach the learning and the tongue of the Chaldeans"* (Daniel 1:2-3).

When Daniel showed up in Babylon, he *"...purposed in his heart that he would not defile himself with the portion of the king's meat, nor with the wine which he drank: therefore he requested of the prince of the eunuchs that he might not* *defile himself. Now God had brought Daniel into **favor** and tender love with the prince of the eunuchs*" (Daniel 1:8-9).

It was Daniel's integrity and purposefulness that shaped His trans-generational favor. He went from a counsellor to Kings' Nebuchadnezzar and Belshazzar, to becoming the first President under Kings' Dairus and Cyrus. As a result, for seventy years, he walked in an unblemished career path that took him to the zenith of his career.

The secret, however, was his impeccable character and the outcome was irresistible favor. In Daniel 6:3-4, the Bible says "*…Daniel was **preferred** above the presidents and princes, because an **excellent** spirit was in him; and the king thought to set him over the whole realm. Then the presidents and princes sought to find occasion against Daniel concerning the kingdom; but they could find none occasion nor fault; forasmuch as he was **faithful**, neither was there any error or fault found in him.*"

FAVOR DOES NOT FOLLOW WORDS; IT FOLLOWS THE WILL!

It is not only the words you speak that makes people like you, but how determined your will is! In Proverbs 16:7, the wise man said "*when a man's ways please the LORD, he maketh even his enemies to be at peace with him.*" When a believer's will is set on God, not man, favor follows!

In Daniel 1:8, the Bible says Daniel "*…purposed in his heart…*" before he became the preferred eunuch who "*God…brought Daniel into **favor** and tender love with the prince of the* eunuchs" (Daniel 1:9). The result of this was that "*...in all matters of wisdom and understanding, that the king enquired of them, he found them ten times better than all the magicians and astrologers that were in all his realm*" (Daniel 1:20).

Those who endure to the end will be saved, or in other words, find favor with God. Too many quit before they see their favor! Too many believers quit just before their breakthrough unaware that favor has a set time for manifestation. In Psalm 102:13, the Psalmist says "*thou shalt arise, and have mercy upon Zion: for the time to favor her, yea, the set time, is come.*" When you hold out for God's salvation, and not some cheap substitute, it births the set time for favor upon your life.

Quitters never win and winners never quit. Your favor is around the corner but will you wait for it to manifest is the question. In Hebrews 6:11-12, the author of Hebrews says "*...every one of you* (should) *show the same diligence to the full assurance of hope unto the end that ye be not slothful, but followers of them who through faith and patience inherit the promises.*"

THE ROAD TO GREATNESS

Daniel did not become great because he belonged to every clique or cult there was. He became great because he stuck to divine purpose, amid peer and palace pressure. In Daniel 1:8, "*Daniel purposed in his heart that he would not defile himself with the portion of the king's meat, nor with the wine which he drank: therefore he requested of the prince of the eunuchs that he might not defile himself.*"

Daniel reigned as president in three consecutive Babylonian administrations because God made him great by divine salesmanship. God can raise your value so high man cannot diminish it because He alone can take you where grace cannot keep you. Man, on the other hand, takes you where they cannot stop you from falling.

The benefit of the way of Christ is that it is clean with mountain raising and non-climaxing effect. In Psalm 19:9, the Psalmist says, "*the fear of the LORD is clean, enduring forever....*" It rides the storm to bring you down at the head of the corner in everlasting triumph.

God achieves His ultimate aim of productivity and profit, alongside worship to God and without wickedness to men, through *gracing favor*. That is why, in Daniel 11:32, God said "*...such as do wickedly against the covenant shall he corrupt by flatteries: but the people that do know their God shall be strong, and do exploits.*"

TURNED CAREFULLY, AND TWIN CHILDREN!

My wife and I waited 15 years to have our own children. It was a challenging life situation that had taken us across the United States in search of answers from doctors and pastors, but to no avail. On one of our Holy Ghost Night prayer meetings, in 2017, the Holy Spirit invaded the room and said "*...seek me with all your heart, and you will find me.*"

Even though, I was leading the prayer meeting I retreated into a corner of the hotel ballroom, and began to cry, seek, and pray unto God. A few months later, specifically on January 28th, 2018, a phone call came telling us that twin children had been born at a hospital in Enugu, Nigeria with no willing parents and asked if I and my wife were prepared to adopt them.

After meeting the necessary requirements, my wife and I adopted the children and today they are our biological children as Momahs.' Even while believing God for our own biological children, we see these as a token of God's faithfulness and a fulfillment of his Word to make us a father and mother of our own children. Selah

Prayer: Every servant riding the horse of your destiny somersault and die, in Jesus name

***You cannot live before you die
if you never died in this life!***

—Tobe Momah M.D.

CHAPTER SEVENTEEN

JOB: A PROFILE IN GRACING FAVOR

> *"Thou hast clothed me with skin and flesh, and hast fenced me with bones and sinews. Thou hast granted me life and **favor**, and thy visitation hath preserved my spirit. And these things hast thou hid in thine heart: I know that this is with thee"* (Job 10:11-13).

In Job 10:12, the wealthiest man in the East named Job testified that God *"...hast granted me **life** and **favor**, and thy visitation hath preserved my spirit."* He was a spellbinding success in his day, but the root cause were the twin powers of grace and favor. It was God's divine grace that brought him spiritual life, and His favor that attracted him wealth beyond measure!

Even though already the wealthiest man of his time (Job 1:3), Job doubled his wealth within an average of ten years to become probably the wealthiest person of his era. The secret was not shaming, blaming and renaming as some are wont to do today but forgiveness, favor and focusing on God.

In Job 42:10-12, the Bible says "...*the L*ORD *turned the captivity of Job, when he prayed for his friends: also the L*ORD *gave Job twice as much as he had before. Then came there unto him all his brethren, and all his sisters, and all they that had been of his acquaintance before, and did eat bread with him in his house: and they bemoaned him, and comforted him over all the evil that the L*ORD *had brought upon him: every man also gave him a piece of money, and everyone an earring of gold. So the L*ORD *blessed the latter end of Job more than his beginning.*"

It was this **Gracing favor** kind of breakthrough that was responsible for Job's exponential manifestation of God's glory! In 2 Corinthians 9:8-11, the Bible says "...*God is able to make all **grace** abound toward you; that ye, always having **all sufficiency in all things**, may abound to every good work: (As it is written, He hath dispersed abroad; he hath given to the poor: his righteousness remaineth for ever. Now he that ministereth seed to the sower both minister bread for your food, and multiply your seed sown, and increase the fruits of your righteousness;) Being **enriched in everything** to all bountifulness, which causeth through us thanksgiving to God.*"

JOB'S JAMBOREE

Job attributed his *wealthiest in the east* status to the power of the dew. He said, "...*my root was spread out by the waters, and the **dew** lay all night upon my branch. My glory was **fresh** in me, and my bow was renewed in my hand*" (Job 29:19-20).

The dew represents the anointing (Psalm 133:3), and the bow represents strength. Job, in his prime, returned to his secret place on a daily basis to get fresh oil and renewed strength. Notwithstanding the pain of his trials and sickness, Job remained strong in faith (Job 19:25) and refused to speak evil of God (Job 1:22; Job 2:10).

In Psalm 92:10-14, the Psalmist said, "*...my horn shalt thou exalt like the horn of an unicorn: I shall be anointed with **fresh** oil. Mine eye also shall see my desire on mine enemies, and mine ears shall hear my desire of the wicked that rise up against me. The righteous shall **flourish** like the palm tree: he shall grow like a cedar in Lebanon. Those that be planted in the house of the* LORD *shall flourish in the courts of our God. They shall still bring forth fruit in old age; they shall be **fat** and flourishing.*"

These fat ones are those who keep the oil fresh! They have "*...wine that maketh glad the heart of man, oil to make his face to shine, and bread which strengtheneth man's heart*" (Psalm 104:15). The anointing was the reason for Job's success. As a result, he asked "*is not my help in me? and is wisdom driven quite from me?*" (Job 6:13).

It was the anointing of the Holy Spirit that raised him, kept him, and made him so great that when he "*...went out to the gate through the city,* (and)*...prepared* (his)*...seat in the street, the young men saw me, and hid themselves: and the aged arose, and stood up. The princes refrained talking, and laid their hand on their mouth. The nobles held their peace, and their tongue cleaved to the roof of their mouth. When the ear heard me, then it blessed me; and when the eye saw me, it gave witness to me:...* (so that) *the blessing of him that was ready to perish came upon me: and I caused the widow's heart to sing for joy*" (Job 29:7-13).

FAVOR LESS NESS FOLLOWS THE UNFORGIVING!

Many favor less lives are because their love relationship has ended! While afflicted, and riddled with boils, Job lamented and said *"my breath is strange to my wife, though I intreated for the children's sake of mine own body"* (Job 19:17).

His wife had earlier on said to him, *"dost thou still retain thine integrity? curse God, and die"* (Job 2:9). To this blasphemous statement, Job had replied saying, *"… thou speakest as one of the foolish women speaketh…what? shall we receive good at the hand of God, and shall we not receive evil?…"* (Job 2:10).

Job, however, did not let his wife's behavior make him bitter or critical. He knew that *"…a man of wicked devices is hated"* (Proverbs 14:17). If Job had been unforgiving, he would not have seen his divine restoration (see Job 42:10-12). He, therefore, forgave his wife and his acquaintances and as a result he got double for his trouble.

In Job 42:7-9, God told Job's friends *"…my wrath is kindled against thee, and against thy two friends: for ye have not spoken of me the thing that is right, as my servant Job hath. Therefore take unto you now seven bullocks and seven rams, and go to my servant Job, and offer up for yourselves a burnt offering; and my servant Job shall pray for you: for **him will I accept**: lest I deal with you after your folly, in that ye have not spoken of me the thing which is right, like my servant Job. So Eliphaz the Temanite and Bildad the Shuhite and Zophar the Naamathite went, and did according as the LORD commanded them: the LORD also accepted Job."*

It took favor to make others bring money to Job, and grace to bring him to twice as much as he had before his affliction (Job 42:11-12), but before that he had to show love to even the most un loveable and forgive those some would consider unforgiveable.

My UMMC Promotion

I started at the University of Mississippi Medical Center in February 2017, after been the medical director at a Federally Qualified Health Center (FQHC) in Louisiana, with the ambition of becoming a full professor in a couple of years. I was inundated with several viewpoints, including those who felt it was unattainable having come from a third world country, and no past United States academic experience.

I persisted, however, having been given a God-given goal to attain this objective within a certain timeline. I published about twenty scientific publications, presented at various fora, and after four years, applied for promotion. In December 2021, I was told that I had tentatively been accepted to go from Assistant professor to associate professor.

It was the fulfillment of a dream I had had since medical school. I had, even while in 2nd year of medical school, signed my books *Professor Tobe Momah* believing that *"faithful is he that calleth you, who also will do it"* (I Thessalonians 5:24). Today more than thirty years after, I can look back and state that it has been *"…not by might, nor by power, but by* (His)*…spirit…"* (Zechariah 4:7). Praise God!

Prayer: Remember my life with thy grace and favor, in Jesus name!

*If you don't want your life
to be a secret, better find out
the secrets of your life!*

—Tobe Momah M.D.

CHAPTER EIGHTEEN

JESUS: A PROFILE IN GRACING FAVOR

*"And Jesus increased in wisdom and stature, and in **favor** with God and man"* (Luke 2:52),

Our Lord and master, Jesus Christ, is an epitome of *gracing favor*. He was a beneficiary of favor and divine grace, and even at the age of twelve, "...*increased in wisdom and stature, and in **favor** with God and man*" (Luke 2:52). If Jesus, the Son of God, needed favor on the earth, you and I need it even more!

In Hebrews 5:7, while facing one of the most arduous moments of his life, Jesus leaned on Divine grace and favor to fulfill the ministry of bringing many sons to glory (Hebrews 2:10) that God had earmarked for him. It says, Jesus *"who in the days of his flesh, when he had offered up prayers and **supplications** with strong crying and tears unto him that was able to save him from death, and was heard in that he feared"* (Hebrews 5:7).

The word translated *supplications*, in the above verse, is the Greek word *hiketeria*. It means approaching or **entreating for a favor**. It means, therefore, that Jesus was heard because He wanted engagement with the Father. He wanted the real, and not a ruse; He was determined to get the substance and not the shadow, and so sought God accordingly!

JESUS CHRIST VERSUS JOHN THE BAPTIST

A critical difference between the ministry of Jesus Christ and that of John the Baptist was the absence of favor in the latter and the preponderance of favor with the former. For example, Jesus was given the upper room fully furnished for the last supper free by the owner (Luke 22:12), given the donkey to ride into Jerusalem with freely (Mark 11:1-6), had boats given to him for ministry (Luke 5:3), foods donated to the ministry (John 6:9-11), invited for dinners (Luke 7:36), and had ministry supporters that shouldered his ministry costs (Luke 8:3). John, on the other hand, was never offered any of these.

Both were endued with the spirit of God from birth, but compared to Jesus, John lacked favor. While John, "*…grew, and waxed strong in spirit, and was in the deserts till the day of his shewing unto Israel*" (Luke 1:80), Jesus "*…grew, and waxed strong in spirit, filled with wisdom: and the* **grace** *of God was upon him*" (Luke 2:40).

It was that grace that opened doors for the future favor Jesus had with God and man. In Luke 2:52, the Bible says "*…Jesus increased in wisdom and stature, and* **in favor** *with God and man.*" This Gracing Favor eventually eclipsed John's ministry, and enabled Jesus to open the double cleaved gates and return with the power of the spirit of God from the wilderness (Luke 4:14).

Jesus came full of grace, mercy and truth (John 1:16-17), but John came with violence and force (Matthew 11:11-12). The lack of grace and favor can lead to a beleaguered, shuttered, and sheltered lifestyle, like John the Baptist had. Favor, on the other hand, carries impact, causes dynamism, changes stories, and overturns obstacles. It can take a zero (like Esther or Daniel) and turn them into heroes of their days.

THE GRACE TO SACRIFICE!

The sacrifice of the saint is the only acceptable offering before God the father. This sacrifice is facilitated by grace, and consummated by favor. In Galatians 2:20-21, Apostle Paul said *"I am crucified with Christ: nevertheless I live; yet not I, but Christ liveth in me: and the life which I now live in the flesh I live by the faith of the Son of God, who loved me, and gave himself for me. I do not frustrate the **grace of God:....**"*

The meaning of the above scripture is that without Grace it is impossible to be sacrificed and live by the faith of Jesus Christ. When Jesus was on earth, He also mad a sacrifice of his life for sin. He said, *"...I come (in the volume of the book it is written of me,) to do thy will, O God. Above when he said, Sacrifice and offering and burnt offerings and offering for sin thou wouldest not, neither hadst pleasure therein; which are offered by the law; Then said he, Lo, I come to do thy will, O God..."* (Hebrews 10:7-10).

There is a grace for sacrifice, but it can frustrated or fulfilled. If you reject or dis esteem divine help, you will make an offering that God has no pleasure or favor in. If you have respect unto the covenant, on the other hand, the termination of the cruel and dark places of the earth beckons. In Psalm 74:20, the Psalmist prays that the Church "*have respect unto the covenant: for the dark places of the earth are full of the habitations of cruelty.*"

BIEDENHARN'S BILLIONS VIA BOTTLING!

Tucked in the wooded area of Monroe, Louisiana overlooking the Quachita river is the Biedenharn Coca-Cola Museum. A collection of relics from the past, it chronicles the journey of the Biedenharn family from Vicksburg, Mississippi (MS) to Monroe, Louisiana (La) and how Joseph Biedenharn started the bottling revolution by bottling Coca-Cola in 1894.

After a pharmacist, John Pemberton, had discovered the coca-cola drink in 1866 it was sold in fountains at local Chemists. When approached, at his Vicksburg, MS store, by a marketing agent for Coca-Cola (Mr. Chandler) to consider bottling Coca-Cola, Mr. Joseph Biedenharn jumped at the opportunity. He said to himself, *why not bottle it for our country trade and sell it for 10 cents above our price of 60 cents for the bottled soda water?*

The rest, as they say, is history! Joseph Biedenharn started a bottling plant in Vicksburg, MS and later opened another one in Monroe, La. He made about 15 cents on every bottle of coke sold, and the more he sold the larger his profits. It was a matter of years before the bottled soda overtook the dispensed soda from HIS Chemist, and with that Mr Biedenharn's wealth multiplied.

He went on to open a crop-duster airline, with other investors, and that airline is today the world's largest passenger airline - Delta airlines. For years, the headquarters of the airline was in Monroe, La before been relocated to Atlanta, Georgia. In fact, its commencement flight flew from Dallas, Texas to Jackson, MS through Monroe, LA in 1929, and it has since grown to become a most formidable airline.

Eventually, Mr Biedenharn moved to Monroe, La and in 1914 opened his quintessential residence in the Monroe garden estate. His daughter, Emy-Lou, took up a fascination with collecting Bibles and singing. Today, that residence houses a Bible and Coca-Cola Museum, and is evident of a heritage rich in faith and bridled with favor.

Prayer: Stir up within me the Spirit of good understanding, might, and favor in Jesus Name!

PART III

Pathways to Gracing Favor

- **Shout**
- **Stand**
- **Sight**
- **Supplication**
- **Surrender**
- **Situate**
- **Service**
- **Shed love**
- **Swiftness**
- **Sincerity**
- **Stirrings**

*Watch what you say, they become thoughts.
Watch what you think, they become actions!*

CHAPTER NINETEEN

SHOUT

> *"Behold, I have received commandment to bless: and he hath blessed; and I cannot reverse it. He hath not beheld iniquity in Jacob, neither hath he seen perverseness in Israel: the LORD his God is with him, and the **shout of a king is among them**. God brought them out of Egypt; he hath as it were the strength of an unicorn. Surely there is no enchantment against Jacob,..."* (Numbers 23:20-24).

Those who have the **Gracing Favor** of the Lord must have the shout of the King within them! They are not ashamed to declare the name of the Lord, but speak with boldness when called upon to do so. They are the ones spoken of by the Psalmist, in Psalm 107:2, when he said *"let the redeemed of the LORD say so, whom he hath redeemed from the hand of the enemy."*

In Numbers 23:21-23, the prophet Balaam said God "...*hath not beheld iniquity in Jacob, neither hath he seen perverseness in Israel: the LORD his God is with him, and the **shout of a king** is among them* (but) *God brought them out of Egypt;* (and) *hath as it were the strength of an unicorn. Surely there is no enchantment against Jacob, neither is there any divination against Israel: according to this time it shall be said of Jacob and of Israel, What hath God wrought!*"

God abides where the shout of a King lives! These ones cannot be enchanted, as long as they speak the Word of God loud and long. In Isaiah 45:3-4, Cyrus was commissioned to receive "...*the treasures of darkness, and hidden riches of secret places, that thou mayest know that I, the LORD, which call thee by thy name, am the God of Israel* (and) *for Jacob my servant's sake, and Israel mine elect, I have even called thee by thy name: **I have surnamed thee**, though thou hast not known me.*"

When God surnames an individual, it means He has given you flattering titles or surnamed you after Himself. Queen Esther, and the people of Israel, would have perished if Queen Esther had refused to shout her identity as a Jew from the rooftops. Her courage to scream His word set her on the path to **Gracing Favor** (Esther 2:17) that changed her *status quo* and placed Israel in influence for generations to come.

THE SPIRIT OF FAITH SPEAKS, NOT SHUTS UP!

When a believer truly believes, there will be a shout not a whimper. In 2 Corinthians 4:13-15, Apostle Paul says "we *having the same spirit of faith, according as it is written, I believed, and therefore have I spoken; we also* *believe, and therefore speak; Knowing that he which raised up the Lord Jesus shall raise up us also by Jesus, and shall present us with you. For all things are for your sakes, that the **abundant grace** might through the thanksgiving of many redound to the glory of God."*

There is no true shout of faith without *gracing favor* at work! It is what you say that determines the flow of favor away or towards you. In Proverbs 16:13, the wise man said *"righteous lips are the delight of kings; and they love him that speaketh right."*

Before Job's restoration, to double of his earlier held blessings, God reprimanded his friends – Eliphaz, Bildad and Zophar – saying *"my wrath is kindled against thee, and against thy two friends: for ye have **not spoken** of me the thing that is right, as my servant Job hath"* (Job 42:7).

They had to bring an offering of *"…seven bullocks and seven rams, and go to my servant Job, and offer up for yourselves a burnt offering; and my servant Job shall pray for you: for him will I accept: lest I deal with you after your folly, in that ye have **not spoken of me the thing which is right, like my servant Job**"* (Job 42:8).

The faith that births **Gracing Favor** and enshrines *double for your trouble* is the faith that speaks right words. It does not speak out of coincidence, or convenience but in confidence! As they do, favor and grace follows them.

In 1 Peter 3:10, Apostle Peter says that *"he that will love life, and see good days, let him refrain his tongue from evil, and his lips that they speak no guile:"* The Psalmist adds, in Psalm 50:23, that *"…him that ordereth his conversation aright will I shew the salvation of God."*

LIFTING WORDS!

There are words that lift, and there are words that lower a man or woman to the grave. When words are building and encouraging, they are lifting words but when they weary, tear down, demoralize and flagellate they are lowering words. The wise man, in Proverbs 18:20-21, said *"a man's belly shall be satisfied with the fruit of his mouth; and with the increase of his lips shall he be filled. Death and life are in the power of the tongue: and they that love it shall eat the fruit thereof."*

The Lord asked the people of Israel to beware of such lowering words in Isaiah 8:11-13. He said, God spoke, *"...to me with a strong hand, and instructed me that I should not walk in the way of this people, saying, say ye not, A confederacy, to all them to whom this people shall say, a confederacy; neither fear ye their fear, nor be afraid. Sanctify the LORD of hosts himself; and let him be your fear, and let him be your dread."*

The result of this change in speech was that God became *"...a sanctuary* (for them),*...and a stone of stumbling and...a rock of offence to both the houses of Israel, for a gin and for a snare to the inhabitants of Jerusalem. And many among them shall stumble, and fall, and be broken, and be snared, and be taken"* (Isaiah 8:14-15).

The rabidly saved are the right speakers, and the afflicted are the aberrant speakers! In Job 22:29, Eliphaz states a rule in their time which became a template for Job's success. He says, *"when men are cast down, then thou shalt say, there is lifting up; and he shall save the humble person."*

What you say determines what you see! In Proverbs 15:5, the wise man said "*a wholesome tongue is a tree of life but perverseness is a breach in the spirit*" The word interpreted for *wholesome* is derived from the Hebrew word *rapha*, and it means to cure, completely deliver, heal, remedy, and be sound.

Until a man or woman's words change, there will be a continual breach in their spirit by the forces of darkness. You cannot have what you speak against, and you cannot stop what your mouth shouts for! It is what you respect that you attract, and only positive speech births a powerful status.

MISSIONS MONEY AND BILLS BROUHAHA!

Our mission trip to Kano, Nigeria was one of our most challenging ones yet. We were behind budget, our medications had not been supplied in the quantity we normally anticipated, our families were against the trip citing frequent spurts of violence there, and there were no Christian ministries to collaborate with.

After arriving Nigeria, and talking things through with my family we got into Kano late in the evening. An earlier sent emissary, who had been sent to pick us up, was nowhere to be found and we had to take a Taxi to the guest house we had secured before arrival.

On arrival, we were received by our hosts and asked how much money we had budgeted and what medications we brought with us. In a room full of Alhajis, and academics of the other faith, my wife and I told them we had a limited amount of money and drugs and hoped that would suffice for the three days of the program.

They were aghast, and after talking amongst themselves, the chief host foisted a bill of 1.2 million naira on his University to cover the cost of the medications. The program went on without a hitch, and at the end, as we departed the academicians amongst our hosts thanked us for coming.

They stated that they were so sure we were fake physicians and public health officers, that they looked up our profiles when the Missions money was short of what they expected. At the end of the day, however, they saw the love of God through my wife and I, and we were able to jettison the shame of insufficiency. That attitude was what won them over!

Prayer: I purpose to enter through the 2-leaved gates of Grace and favor, in Jesus name, now in Jesus name!

If you stand for nothing, you will fall for anything!

— Tobe Momah M.D.

CHAPTER TWENTY

STAND

"Arise, shine; for thy light is come, and the glory of the LORD is risen upon thee. For, behold, the darkness shall cover the earth, and gross darkness the people: but The LORD shall arise upon thee, and his glory shall be seen upon thee. And the Gentiles shall come to thy light, and kings to the brightness of thy rising" (Isaiah 60:1-3).

Take a stand for Jesus in faith, and unparalleled favor merged with Grace will collide with you eventually. In the case of Joseph, despite been sold by his brothers, scandalized by Potiphar's wife, and forgotten by the baker he stood on the Word of God without equivocation or compromise, and eventually was not only vindicated but also victorious.

In Genesis 39:4-6, the Bible says *"...Joseph found **grace** in his* (Potiphar's) *sight, and he served him: and he made him overseer over his house, and all that he had he put* *into his hand…and he knew not ought he had, save the bread which he did eat. And Joseph was a goodly person, and **well favored**."*

This *gracing favor* was obtained by Joseph, even after he had been betrayed by his siblings, because he took a stand for the Word. In Psalm 105:17-20, the Bible says God "…*sent a man before them, even Joseph, who was sold for a servant whose feet they hurt with fetters: he was laid in iron:* **Until the time that his word came***: the word of the* LORD *tried him. The king sent and loosed him; even the ruler of the people, and let him go free."*

ARISE AND SHINE

In Psalm 102:13-15, God said He will "*…arise and have mercy upon Zion: for the time to favor her, yea, the set time, is come. For thy servants take pleasure in her stones, and favor the dust thereof. So the heathen shall fear the name of the* LORD*, and all the kings of the earth thy glory."*

The word, *arise*, is the Hebrew Word *Qum* and it means to *stand or stir up*! It was the standing or arising of God that spurred the clock of favor to tick for Zion in Psalm 102:13. This same Hebrew word, *Qum*, is used in Isaiah 60:1, where God commands the Church to *"arise,* (and) *shine; for thy light is come, and the glory of the* LORD is risen upon thee."

What, unfortunately, keeps the time of favor or glorification prolonged is the lack of a stand or an arising. God cried out, in Isaiah 64:7, saying "…*there is none that calleth upon thy name, that* **stirreth** *up himself to* **take hold of thee***: for thou hast hid thy face from us, and hast consumed us, because of our iniquities."*

Favor is a function of proximity (James 4:8), and without a stirring or a stand, God is far from the individual. When God stands for you, however, favor is inevitable! In Psalm 84:11, the Psalmist said "*...the LORD God is a sun and shield: the LORD will give* **grace and glory:** *no good thing will he withhold from them that walk uprightly*" Those who walk upright, get the grace and the glory that only God can give, *aka gracing favor*.

SUPERNATURAL STRENGTH

One of the pillars for gracing favor is supernatural strength! Not man-made strength, but divine strength. When God is the source of a man or woman's strength, favor must follow! In Psalm 30:7, the Psalmist prayed saying "*...LORD, by thy favor thou hast made my mountain to stand strong:*"

That is why, in Psalm 89:17, the Psalmist said "*...thou* (God) *art the* **glory** *of their* **strength***: and in thy* **favor** *our horn shall be exalted.*" Without supernatural strength, grace and favor are void. In Zechariah 10:12, God made a promise that He "*...will strengthen them in the LORD; and they shall walk up and down in his name, saith the LORD*" (Zechariah 10:12).

The aftermath of this divine impartation of strength is an "*open...door that* (makes) *the fire...devour cedars*" (Zechariah 11:1)! An open door is the signature *sine-qua-non* for *gracing favor*, but this is impossible without strength or taking a stand!

In Isaiah 60:10-11, the Bible says "*the sons of strangers shall* **build up thy walls***, and their kings shall minister unto thee: for in my wrath I smote thee, but in* **my favor** *have I had*

mercy on thee. Therefore thy gates shall be open continually...."
Until you are built up, and take a stand, you are bereft of favor and mercy and instead of open gates, you hit the closed gates.

THE TALE OF TWO LANDLORDS

My wife and I rented our homes in Brooklyn, NY, Ruston, La, Pineville, La, and West Monroe La until we finally decided to buy our current home in 2016. Till then, we were at the mercy of the vagaries among landlords and we definitely had our fair share of them.

After leaving Ruston, Louisiana, I got a job at the Angola prisons in St Francisville Louisiana, and the nearest place of abode that would allow my wife continue her studies at Louisiana State University (LSU), Shreveport and permit my work schedule while in Central Louisiana was Pineville, La. After looking at properties there, we signed a lease for a year with a landlord for a property in Pineville.

After only seven months on the job, however, the Angola prison offer of a job was abruptly terminated and I had to quickly relocate to Monroe, La for work. As a result, my wife and I made trips up there on the weekends in search of a house. We still attended Church in West Monroe, La and it afforded us the opportunity to scout properties in the area.

On one of those Sunday afternoons, after the Sunday morning service, my wife and I were with our Pastor (Shane Warren) in his home and just before they were about to start evening growth group fellowship, I felt the need to leave. I told my wife, and after checking with my Pastor, we took our leave.

Before heading to Pineville, however, the Holy Spirit led me to take some back roads we had never taken before. As we turned into a dead end, we saw a gentleman and his wife leaving a signage *for rent* in the yard of a house. These couple would go on to be our landlord and landlady for five years and they treated us like a gem.

On the other hand, the Pineville landlord made our lives so miserable. When we were ready to re-locate from Pineville, and after explaining to him the sudden termination and how short our finances were, he still insisted on collecting every penny due to him for the remaining five months of the one year lease.

He threatened us with court actions, if we did not comply, and eventually I had to take money from my father, late General Sam Momah, to help offset the balance of nearly seven thousand dollars. That experience spurred my wife and I to start praying a prayer for favor on a daily basis, and truly since then it has been *gracing favor* all the way!

Prayer: Let your hand be upon me for Good, O Lord, in Jesus name!

*If the gods want to kill a man,
they first make him blind!*

—Local African proverb

CHAPTER TWENTY-ONE

SIGHT

> *"Good understanding giveth **favor** but the way of transgressors is hard"* (Proverbs 13:15).

Those who want grace and favor must have insight and revelation first. In Proverbs 13:15, the wise man says *"good understanding giveth favor but the way of transgressors is hard."* It is a lack of revelation that stops the radiance or *gracing favor* of the believer. Those who see shine, but those who are deaf are darkened.

In Proverbs 8:33-35, the wise man said *"hear instruction, and be wise, and refuse it not. Blessed is the man that heareth me, watching daily at my gates, waiting at the posts of my doors. For whoso findeth me findeth life, and shall **obtain favor** of the Lord."*

It is your **discovery that makes for your distinction!** In Proverbs 25:2, the wise man said *"it is the glory of God to conceal a thing: but the honor of kings is to search out a matter."* The word used for *Honor* is the word *Kabowd*, and it means to be glorious or have weighty influence.

Until the "...*eyes of your understanding* (are)... *enlightened;...ye may* (not) *know what is the hope of his calling, and what the riches of the glory of his inheritance in the saints* (are), *and what is the exceeding greatness of his power to us-ward who believe, according to the working of his mighty power*" (Ephesians 1:18-19), we remain moribund.

THE LIGHT OF THY COUNTENANCE

There must be insight before an invigorating of *gracing favor*! In Psalm 44:3, the Psalmist said the Israelite "...*got not the land in possession by their own sword, neither did their own arm save them: but thy right hand, and thine arm, and the **light** of thy countenance, because thou hadst a **favor** unto them.*"

Before the favor that gave Israel the promised land, the Lord had to be the light of their countenance. When God is the light of your countenance, darkness is obliterated and sight is restored. The result of this keen insight is Grace and favor. When Moses "...*turn*(ed) *aside,* (to) *see this great sight, why the bush is not burnt*" (Genesis 3:3), the portals of favor opened unto him and gave him unparalleled power to bring the Israelites out of Egypt.

In Deuteronomy 33:13-17, Moses recollected this encounter in his blessing of Joseph. He said, "*Blessed of the LORD be his land...and for **the good will** (or favor) of him that dwelt in the bush: let the blessing come upon the head of Joseph, and upon the top of the head of him that was separated from his brethren. His glory is like the firstling of his bullock, and his horns are like the horns of unicorns: with them he shall push the people together to the ends of the earth....*"

Insight always precedes input, and revelation resources. **It takes an unveiling to capture the invaluable, and precision to acquire the precious.** That is why, in Job 17:4, Job said *"thou hast hid their heart from understanding: therefore shalt thou not exalt them."*

ONE HUNDRED AND FIFTY THREE

The Apostle Peter was so disillusioned after the death and crucifixion of Jesus, he and the other five disciples with him could not even recognize Jesus. In John 21:4, the Bible says, after a futile night of fishing, *"…the morning was now come,* (and) *Jesus stood on the shore but the disciples **knew not** that it was Jesus."*

The disciple Jesus loved later recognized Jesus (John 21:7), after he told them to *"…cast the net on the right side of the ship, and…they cast therefore, and…were not able to draw it for the multitude of fishes"* (John 21:6). They, after he recognized Jesus, brought in *"…**an hundred and fifty and three** (fish) and…there were so many, yet was not the net broken"* (John 21:11).

In Hebrew Numerology, 153 means grace and mercy that stands between man and God. Before there is *gracing favor*, sight must be sharp and clarity must be clear! The aftermath of a life blessed with Gracing favor is demonstrated by the 153 fish who despite been large and numerous did not break the net.

The new normal in the last days will be a *gracing favor* that grants **Favor to Get, and Grace to stand**! The nets of *gracing favor* will never break, no matter the pressure! They are undergirded by the Holy Spirit, who raised the Lord Jesus Christ from the dead (Romans 8:11), and the "*God* (who) *is able to make all grace abound…that…always having all sufficiency in all things,* (we) *may abound* (un)*to every good work*" (2 Corinthians 9:8).

FACING FEAR FEARLESSLY!

I was attending Mountain of Fire and Miracles Ministries, Lagos Nigeria while working as an intern at the military hospital, Lagos. At the time, I was staying at a government guest house and on my way back from a Sunday evening Church service, I met armed robbers in action at the reception of the guest house.

On that fateful morning, I had heard God's gentle whisper tell me *I will cover you*. Even though I had three menacing, revolver-handling men around me, I had no fear at all.

The cold nose of their gun was struck to my temple, and I was ordered to give them my car keys and every other valuable I had on me. They took all my cash, my watch, and even my gold rimmed glasses.

Hoping to make a get away with it, they asked me to lead them to my car. On arriving at my car, however, they couldn't find the car keys. There had been a power outage before my arrival at the guest house and as a result, search as they might, they couldn't find the car keys.

They eventually ran away with another near by vehicle. After their departure, I found my keys right where they had been looking for them. God had covered the keys from them and reserved them for me in fulfillment of His word to me that morning.

Unfortunately for the owner of the robbers' get-way car, their car was found in a neighboring West African country dilapidated and vandalized. Like the old hymnal song, all I could recite when I heard the aftermath of the robbery, was *but for grace, there goes I*!

Prayer: I receive grace for marathon favors, in Jesus name!

Prayer Moves the Hand that Moves the World.

—Aikman John Wallace
(1802 – 1870)
Scottish Free Church Minister

CHAPTER TWENTY-TWO

SUPPLICATIONS

> "...*Thou art my Son, today have I begotten thee. As he saith also in another place, thou art a priest for ever after the order of Melchisedec. Who in the days of his flesh, when he had offered up prayers and **supplications** with strong crying and tears unto him that was able to save him from death, and was heard in that he feared*;" (Hebrews 5:5-7).

The priest Ezra was faced by a corruption of the holy seed by the priests, levites, and leaders of the peoples after he had brought the remnant back to Jerusalem. Instead of moaning and mumbling, he took to supplication, fasting, and prayers to change the story of Israel.

In Ezekiel 9:8-9, Ezra prayed to God saying "...*now for a little space **grace** hath been shewed from the L*ORD *our God, to leave us a remnant to escape, and to give us a nail in his holy place, that our God may lighten our eyes, and give us a little reviving in our bondage. For we were* *bondmen; yet our God hath not forsaken us in our bondage, but hath extended **mercy** (or favor) unto us in the sight of the kings of Persia, to give us a reviving, to set up the house of our God, and to repair the desolations thereof, and to give us a wall in Judah and in Jerusalem."*

As a result of Ezra's prayers and supplications, *"…the fierce wrath of God for this matter* (was)…*turned from* (them)…" (Ezra 10:14). Prayer moves the hand of God, and stirs up favor. In Ezra 8:22-23, the Bible says *"…,the hand of our God is upon all them for good that seek him; but his power and his wrath is against all them that forsake him. So we fasted and besought our God for this: and he was intreated of us."*

THE FIGHT THAT BIRTHS FAVORS

Without prayer, Favor is moribund. Before favor showed up in Egypt for the Israelites, God had stretched out His hands and delivered His people in answer to their prayers. In Exodus 3:7-9, God told Moses *"I have surely seen the affliction of my people which are in Egypt, and have heard their **cry** by reason of their taskmasters; for I know their sorrows; And I am come down to deliver them out of the hand of the Egyptians, and to bring them up out of that land unto a good land and a large…now therefore, behold, the cry of the children of Israel is come unto me…."*

In Exodus 3:20-22, He added that as a result of their cry *"…I will stretch out my hand, and smite Egypt with all my wonders which I will do in the midst thereof: and after that he will let you go. And I will give this people **favor** in the sight of the Egyptians: and it shall come to pass, that, when ye go, ye shall not go empty. But every woman shall borrow of* *her neighbor, and of her that sojorneth in her house, jewels of silver, and jewels of gold, and raiment: and ye shall put them upon your sons, and upon your daughters; and ye shall spoil the Egyptians."*

It takes a fight to birth favor, and warfare to be welcomed! Favor requires power from on high to overthrow the enemies holding back the Grace and favor of God over one's life. The Israelites had, in Exodus 2:23-24, *"...sighed by reason of the bondage, and **they cried**, and their cry came up unto God by reason of the bondage. And God heard their groaning, and God remembered his covenant with Abraham, with Isaac, and with Jacob."*

The aftermath of this heartfelt cry by the people of Israel was an unparalleled favor and grace to spoil Egypt and swallow up Pharaoh and his six hundred chariots in the Red sea (Exodus 14:27-28). In Exodus 12:35-36, the Bible says *"...the children of Israel did according to the word of Moses; and they borrowed of the Egyptians jewels of silver, and jewels of gold, and raiment and the* LORD gave the people ***favor*** *in the sight of the Egyptians, so that they lent unto them such things as they required. And they spoiled the Egyptians."*

DOUBLE CAMP, DOUBLE BLESSINGS!

The Patriarch Jacob prayed for favor before he saw his brother Esau. Before he saw his then alienated brother (Esau), *"...Jacob was left alone; and there wrestled a man with him until the breaking of the day....And he said, let me go, for the day breaketh. And* (Jacob) *said, I will not let thee go, except thou bless me"* (Genesis 32:24-26).

The aftermath of this prayer was the blessing of **Gracing Favor** upon Jacob. In Genesis 32:28, the Lord said "*...thy name shall be called no more Jacob, but Israel: for as a prince hast thou power with God and with men, and hast prevailed.*" Favor does not happen without some contention for it!

The place Jacob wrestled with God is a place called *Mahanaim,* which means *double-camp.*" In Genesis 32:1-3, the Bible says "*...Jacob went on his way, and the angels of God met him and when Jacob saw them, he said, this is God's host: and he called the name of that place* **Mahanaim***. And Jacob sent messengers before him to Esau....*"

It was a place of contradictions for Jacob for while there, he faced fear but fought in faith nonetheless (Genesis 32:24-30). He saw terror, but continued in trust nonetheless. He was happy to travel home, but feared the trouble he had stirred up by supplanting his brother, Esau, in Genesis 27:2-38 would consume him.

He sent men to see his brother, and this began a strategy to beat his brother but when he came to the end of himself in Genesis 32:24, he yielded to *gracing favor* and decided to seek God instead. The double gates of grace and favor open to prayer! Jacob wrestled all night, and at the end of his all night prayer, the dispositions with his brother was overtaken by favor. Instead of war, his brother Esau readily welcomed him (see Genesis 33:10-11).

The gates of the double camp of grace and favor are thrown open by supplication. In Psalm 106:4-5, the Psalmist prayed for favor saying "*remember me, O LORD, with the favor that thou bearest unto thy people: O visit me with thy salvation. That I may see the good of thy chosen, that*

I may rejoice in the gladness of thy nation, that I may glory with thine inheritance."

In Hosea 12:3-4, the prophet further elaborates on these blessing and how it was supplication that birthed it. He said, "*He* (Jacob) *took his brother by the heel in the womb, and by his strength he had power with God: Yea, he had power over the angel, and prevailed: he wept, and made* **supplication** *unto him: he found him in Bethel, and there he spake with us."*

JOY DARA: FROM GLORY TO GLORY

Pastor (Dr) Joy Dara is the pastor of the largest church in central Louisiana. He arrived America in 1980 as an undergraduate student, and had to sleep on classroom floors because of limited resources. As a Christian, however, he believed in always being joyful regardless of the circumstance. His philosophy on life stems from James 1:2-4 which says, "*…count it all joy when ye fall into divers temptations. Knowing this, that the trying of your faith works patience. But let patience have her perfect work, that ye may be perfect and entire wanting nothing."*

He excelled in his classroom studies and went on to obtain a Doctor of Jurisprudence (JD) degree from Southern University, Baton Rouge, Louisiana, and Masters of Law degree from the University of Arkansas, Fayetteville, after his Bachelor of Arts degree from California Baptist University, Riverside. As a minister, he served under different denominational leaders as worship leader and assistant pastor. He married, had children; and as he settled into secular life, was invited by a local church to serve as their pastor.

This church, then called Zion Hill Baptist Church, was not growing and had lost two pastors in under a year to mysterious circumstances. The church board that interviewed him pointedly asked him, *"Do you still want the job knowing the previous two occupants died suddenly?"* In his ebullient and unassuming manner, Joy Dara said that he was not afraid of death; and if given the position, he would cause that spirit of death to depart from the church. He took the position as senior pastor and in less than ten years the church increased in leaps and bounds.

The congregation built a state of the art facility that seats over a thousand people, anchored a international television program called "Always Joy" and attracted respect from the community with their innovative programs designed to empower the local population. Dr. Joy Dara currently oversees hundreds of interdenominational ministers and his influence is felt across race, denomination, sex, and age. He has been fondly called the *apostle of always Joy*!

On a recent occasion, while letting a ministry use their facilities, a visiting minister from London, United Kingdom asked for the host pastor. Pastor Dara was not around, and he was reached and brought in to the meeting. With no idea why this visiting minister demanded to see him, Joy Dara walked in unaware his life was about to change forever.

The visiting pastor, there and then, offered him a television recording contract from his international television station in London, UK with slots that would normally cost thousands of dollars free of charge. This led to Joy Dara speaking across the globe from his platform in Pineville, Louisiana.

His life is a testimony of *gracing favor*! He is currently dean of studies at a local Christian university, and has seen his children graduate with distinction in law, pharmacy, and medicine. He is happily married to the wife of his youth, and together they are reaching their world for Christ one soul at a time!

Prayer: I walk through the double gates of grace and favor into my unlimited greatness, in Jesus name!

Favor does not come cheap; it will cost you something!

—Tobe Momah M.D.

CHAPTER TWENTY-THREE

SURRENDER

> *"For thou, LORD, wilt bless the righteous; with **favor** wilt thou compass him as with a shield"* (Psalm 5:12).

The righteous are those God *"...will bless...with **favor**...(that) compass(es)...(them) with a shield"* (Psalm 5:12). These ones have no agenda of their own, but follow a divine agenda. They are surrendered to the will of God, and have given up their selfish goals and passions for His will. They are *surrendered*, and as a result *surrounded by favor*, no matter how dark their circumstances may be.

In Job 11:15-19, the pre-requisite to this sort of Gracing Favor is discussed. It says, *"...(thou) shalt...lift up thy face without spot; yea, thou shalt be stedfast, and shalt not fear: Because thou shalt forget thy misery, and remember it as waters that pass away: And thine age shall be clearer than the noonday:* **thou shalt shine forth**, *thou shalt be as the morning. And thou shalt be secure, because there is hope; yea, thou shalt dig about thee, and thou shalt take thy rest in safety.... yea, many shall make suit unto thee."*

You can't delve in sin, and expect brightness. **A life that is birthed in prayer, and lived in holiness will be fulfilled in favor!** Favor is the *sine qua non* of the Christian life, and it will make you the cynosure of all eyes. There must, however, be a surrender of the individual to God to experience that kind of *gracing favor*. **A clear face is the pathway to current favor**, but it is only available on the platform of steadfastness and surrender.

THE BLESSING PRAYER

When God instituted the blessing prayer in Numbers 6, He intended it as the platform to obtain gracing Favor through a spiritual re-birth! In that prayer, God told Moses to bless Israel saying "...*the LORD bless thee, and keep thee: The LORD make **his face shine** upon thee, and be **gracious** unto thee: The LORD lift up his countenance upon thee, and give thee peace*" (Numbers 6:24-26).

The aftermath of the above prayer was God "...*put*(ting) (His)...*name upon the children of Israel, and...bless*(ing) *them*" (Numbers 6:27). When God shines His name upon you, and is gracious unto you, it is sequel to obtaining His Gracing favor. The aftermath would be his countenance lifted upon you, and His presence and peace encapsulating you forever.

The benefits of Gracing Favor are legendary and life lasting. In Psalm 16:5-6, the Psalmist exclaims that when "*the LORD is the portion of mine inheritance and...maintains* (my) *lot, the lines* (will) *fall...in pleasant places* (and) *yea* (we shall) *have a goodly heritage*" (Psalm 16:5-6).

NO SURRENDER, NO SHINING!

Without surrender to God, you miss out on favor. In Psalm 106:4-5, the Psalmist cried saying *"remember me, O LORD, with the **favo**r that thou bearest unto thy people: O visit me with **thy salvation**; That I may see the good of thy chosen, that I may rejoice in the gladness of thy nation, that I may glory with thine inheritance."*

It is only **His people** that God can bestow His favor upon. He cannot bestow His favor on a rebellious, and a sacrilegious people. He said, in Amos 5:16, to the Church *"hate the evil, and love the good, and establish judgment in the gate: it may be that the LORD God of hosts will be **gracious** unto the remnant of Joseph."*

Today's *hyper-grace* preachers choose to forget the *frustrated grace* preached by Paul in Galatians 2:21. Instead, they concentrate on the *free grace* that comes without a price. God gives favor, but only to a peculiar few; He says, in Psalm 112:5, that *"a good man sheweth **favor**…"* and in Proverbs 12:2 adds that *"a good man obtaineth **favor** of the LORD but a man of wicked devices will he condemn."*

Our last day generation is fraught with many fault lines, in terms of doctrine and philosophy (Luke 21:8, 2 Timothy 3:5-7), and *"…wisdom and knowledge* (must therefore) *be the stability of* (our)*…times, and strength of salvation…"* (Isaiah 33:6). God has given everything needed to reign in life, but it comes on the platter of surrender.

In Romans 5:17, the apostle Paul says that *"…if by one man's offence death reigned by one; much more they which receive abundance of **grace** and of the gift of **righteousness** shall **reign in life** by one, Jesus Christ.)"* You don't have to be intimidated and violated in a world you are supposed to reign over. Receive His gift of righteousness and abundant grace and start to reign over every obstacle in life today.

SAYING FAREWELL!

It was a day I had dreaded for as long as I can remember, but a day I knew would eventually come. Three years before 29th July, 2020 I had told my wife that God was going to take my Dad away, and we must be ready.

She immediately replied *God forbid*, and asked that we embark on fasting and prayers to avert this inevitable end of every man. I encouraged her to go ahead, but as one who had come to recognize God's voice I knew it was not up for discussion or negotiation.

My Dad, late (General) Sam Momah had grown tired after several years battling same and similar illnesses as his father. He had, at least, bettered his father by getting to Seventy seven a few weeks earlier, and every moment of that Birthday had been celebrated locally and globally as if it were his last.

He had been inundated with interviews by the Press hosted to a Birthday party by the family, launched his latest best seller on *Restructuring Nigeria* to rave reviews, and even been a guest of the foremost Television station in the country (National Television Authority) for an exclusive Birthday interview.

Besides the Birthday Bumps, My Dad had done what few before him had ever done! He started a brand new business at fifty-five (post-retirement from the Nigerian Army), took the business to dizzying heights, established a leadership structure that could run without him, and maintained a steady and suitable income for the family and his hundred's of employees.

Compared to his peers, who depended on government largesse, Sam seemed like a genius who planned for retirement years in advance. Internally, though, every day was a struggle for Sam. He wanted to build a legacy, and he would not compromise on the way.

He faced exaggerated bills, epileptic electricity supply, shortage of water, staff disloyalty, fraudulent malpractices and deteriorating health headlong and succeeded (at least in the Nigerian context). He kept his numerous businesses afloat, notwithstanding a hostile economy, and was recognized across political and socio economic stratospheres as an elder statesman.

My greatest regret, however, is I never got to say goodbye. I just wanted to be able to say farewell, and unfortunately I never did. On the day he died, I was beginning my orientation at a new hospital, and while there he called my cellphone asking my brothers and I *put our heads together to checkmate this fever that was re-occurring and damaging his body.*

Before I could reply, however, he had passed without my ever saying goodbye. I called back, cajoling him to go to the hospital but never got his response. By this time, he was non-verbal, distant, and non responsive. Adieu Dad, I hope we see again in the not so distance eternity. I love you, and treasure our times together.

Prayer: Baptize me with God kind of faith that births unparalleled favor in Jesus name!

Your Environment determines your Element, and your Surroundings make for your Settlement!

—Tobe Momah M.D.

CHAPTER TWENTY-FOUR

SITUATE

> "...*the* **grace** *of God that bringeth salvation hath appeared to all men, teaching us that, denying ungodliness and worldly lusts, we should live soberly, righteously, and godly, in this present world; Looking for that blessed hope, and the glorious appearing of the great God and our Savior Jesus Christ*" (Titus 2:11-13).

Where you are situated determines the flow of favor towards or away from you! Who you surround yourself with will determine what surrounds you. When the *Zoe* life of God encompasses you, favor becomes part and parcel of your life because without God's presence, your favor is not verifiable.

His presence is the proof and authentication of His favor on your life. If God goes with you, His favor will also follow you. Favor is God's limitless key to bringing revival, deliverance, and turnaround to the nations.

That is why, in Psalm 30:5-7, He said "...*His anger endureth but a moment; in his **favor is life**:...and in my prosperity I said, I shall never be moved. (for)...by thy favor thou hast made my mountain to stand strong:*"

Many glorious destinies have been destroyed because of poor location! They got entangled with a person or place that beleaguered or belittled their otherwise glorious destiny, and it turned their favor into frustration. In Proverbs 18:22, the wise man said *"whoso findeth a wife findeth a good thing, and obtaineth favor of the LORD."*

The truth is who you join determines what you enjoy, and your environment will determine what element you bring out! In Proverbs 14:9, the wise man again says *"**fools make a mock at sin but among the righteous there is favor**."* Only at His doors of mercy and grace, can **favor** be found. In Proverbs 8:35, he said *"Blessed is the man that heareth me, watching daily at my gates, waiting at the posts of my doors. For whoso find me find life, and shall obtain favor of the LORD."*

FROM CAPTIVES TO CHAMPIONS

The Bible declares, in Proverbs 12:2, that *"a good man obtaineth favor of the LORD but a man of wicked devices will he condemn."* The deeds and environment some people create around themselves are the sole determination for their lack of favor and the nullity of His grace upon their lives. It takes His presence to create an enabling environment for Grace and favor to blossom.

The Psalmist declared this much, in Psalm 116:5-9, when he said, "***gracious*** *is the LORD, and righteous; yea, our God is **merciful**. The LORD preserveth the simple: I was* *brought low, and he helped me. Return unto thy rest, O my soul; for the* LORD *hath dealt bountifully with thee. For thou hast delivered my soul from death, mine eyes from tears, and my feet from falling. I will* **walk before the** LORD *in the land of the living."*

Those who see the bountifulness of the Lord (favor) and taste of his graciousness "...*walk before the* LORD *in the land of the living*" (Psalm 116:9). Every person who wants to taste *gracing favor* must as a matter of priority change location first. They must enter His presence, and experience His unprecedented grace and favor (Psalm 16:11, and Obadiah 17) there.

In the case of Mary, the Angel told her "...*hail, thou that art highly favored, the Lord is with thee*" (Luke 1:28), thus showing the value of location in the quest for favor and Grace. In the case of Joseph, the Bible says "... *the* LORD *was with Joseph, and shewed him mercy, and gave him favor in the sight of the keeper of the prison*" (Genesis 39:21).

RADIATING RESIDENCE!

Apostle Paul portrays the invaluable ness of God's presence to obtaining Gracing favor in his treatise to the Corinthians Church. He unveils this unsurpassed reason for supernatural triumph, to a Church that was fractious, inflamed with carnal passions, and infirmed (spiritually and physically).

In 2 Corinthians 2:14-17, he said "...*thanks be unto God, which always causeth us to triumph in Christ, and maketh manifest the savor of his knowledge by us in every place. For we are unto God a sweet* **savor** *of Christ, in them* *that are saved, and in them that perish: To the one we are the savor of death unto death; and to the other the savor of life unto life. And who is sufficient for these things? For we are not as many, which corrupt the word of God: but as of sincerity, but as of God,* **in the sight of God** *speak we in Christ."*

The word *savor* as used in the above scripture are three Greek words including *Euodia*, *Ozo*, and *Osme*. It is translated *fragrance*, *smell* or *aroma*. It connotes the ability to radiate favor but it is impossible without sincerely speaking in His presence. He says, *"...we are not as many, which corrupt the word of God: but as of sincerity, but as of God, in the sight of God speak we in Christ"* (2 Corinthians 2:17).

Those who stay situated in His presence can be rest assured of His Grace and Favor. In Psalm 5:12, the Bible says *"...the LORD, wilt bless the righteous; with favor wilt thou compass him as with a shield."* The word, *compass*, is the Hebrew Word *atar* and it means to encircle or surround completely. If where you are situated was immaterial, the shield would not seek to encircle one away from the negative influence of a savage world. Selah

THE PRAYER THAT SAVED HUDSON TAYLOR,... AND BIRTHED THE CHINA INLAND MISSION!

At fifteen years of age, Hudson Taylor was a stranger to Christ. He says, *"often I had tried to make myself a Christian and failing, of course, in such efforts, I began at last to think that for some reason or other I could not be saved."* Discouragement caused him to drift to infidelity and waywardness.

One day, when his mother was visiting London, about seventy or eighty miles from home, she stopped by the side of the road determined to pray for her only son until he was born into the heavenly family. For hours she laid hold of the mighty arm of power which surrounds every imperiled soul. And there she remained till she received evidence in her spirit that her son was converted.

In the meantime, while Taylor Hudson's mother travailed in prayer for his soul, his attention was drawn to a little tract in the home library, with the words "*the finished work of Christ,*" emblazoned across it. "*What was finished?*" he questioned; and thus he answered: "*A full and perfect atonement and satisfaction for sin; the debt was paid by the Substitute; Christ died for our sins, and not for ours only, but also for the sins of the whole world.*"

Then came the thought, '*if the whole work was finished and the whole debt paid, what is there left for me to do?*' And with this dawned the joyful conviction, as light flashed into his soul by the Holy Spirit, that there was nothing in the world to be done but to fall down on one's knees, and, accept this Savior and His salvation, and to praise Him forever more.

Being brought up in such a circle and saved under such circumstances, it was natural that from the commencement of Hudson Taylor's spiritual life, he would view prayer as transacting business with God, whether on one's own behalf or on behalf of those for whom one sought His blessing.

He later went on to found the China Inland Mission. A Briton, he gave up everything to pursue his God given dream of being a missionary to China. At the end of his life sojourn, in 1905, the China Inland Mission he had founded had two hundred and five mission stations, eight hundred missionaries, and over one hundred and twenty-five thousand Chinese Christians.

All this would not have been possible if Hudson Taylor's mother had not stopped, and sought God for his soul when he was fifteen years of age, as prompted by the Holy Ghost. Many of life's opportunities are bypassed by people too speedy or unspiritual to connect with the God of the universe.

Prayer: Surround me with your favor as with a Shield, O Lord, in Jesus name!

*The only place you start from
the top is the grave!*

...Ancient African Proverb.

CHAPTER TWENTY-FIVE

SERVICE

> "*...he that in these things **serveth** Christ is acceptable to God, and approved of men*" (Romans 14:18).

Service is a master key to obtaining *gracing favor*. The wise man said, in Proverbs 22:29, that *"seest thou a man diligent in his business? he shall stand before kings; he shall not stand before mean men."*

The instrument of service as a tool for gracing favor was buttressed by Apostle Paul, in Romans 14:17-18. He said, *"...the kingdom of God is not meat and drink; but righteousness, and peace, and joy in the Holy Ghost. For he that in these things **serveth** Christ is acceptable to God, and approved of men."*

Those who serve God will be accepted by God (Grace) and approved of men (favor). Those who live in His gracious favor are avowed servants, not aloof onlookers. They are committed partakers of the kingdom, and not careless parrots who repeat what they hear but don't do what they should do.

David was a major beneficiary from the service toolkit of God. He was described, in Acts 7:46, as one "*…who found **favor** before God, and desired to find a tabernacle for the God of Jacob.*" The favor of God he received for his desire towards God's tabernacle was, however, not in word alone but evident indeed by his service to God.

He said, in 1 Chronicles 29:3-4, "*…I have set my affection to the house of my God, I have of mine own proper good, of gold and silver, which I have given to the house of my God, over and above all that I have prepared for the holy house. Even three thousand talents of gold, of the gold of Ophir, and seven thousand talents of refined silver, to overlay the walls of the houses withal: The gold for things of gold, and the silver for things of silver, and for all manner of work to be made by the hands of artificers. And who then is willing to consecrate his **service** this day unto the LORD?*"

In today's currency, David gave more than twenty billion dollars for a project he had no dream of seeing. He describes his giving as service, and this act was a provoker of the divine favor he carried. This attitude of giving is why He is described in Acts 13:36 as one who "*…had **served** his own generation by the will of God…*"

THE SECRET (CALLED) SERVICE

It takes service to God to shatter dullness and defilement. In Psalm 123:2-3, the Bible says "*…as the eyes of **servants** look unto the hand of their masters, and as the eyes of a maiden unto the hand of her mistress; so our eyes wait upon the LORD our God, until that he have **mercy** upon us. Have mercy upon us, O LORD, have mercy upon us: for we are exceedingly filled with contempt.*"

There is no room to remain in contempt when the mercy (or favor) of God is unveiled. But it will only be poured out on those with the heart of a servant. In Exodus 23:25-27, the Lord said *"ye shall **serve** the LORD your God, and he shall bless thy bread, and thy water; and I will take sickness away from the midst of thee. There shall nothing cast their young, nor be barren, in thy land: the number of thy days I will fulfil."*

Service is a last day hallmark of the last day Church. It is described in Malachi 3:16-18, as the reason why some are jewels and others are jelly. It says *"...they that feared the LORD spake often one to another and the LORD hearkened, and heard it, and a book of remembrance was written before him for them that feared the LORD, and that thought upon his name. And they shall be mine, saith the LORD of hosts, in that day when I make up my **jewel**s; and I will spare them, as a man spareth his own son that serveth him. Then shall ye return, and discern between the righteous and the wicked, between him that **serveth** God and him that serveth him not."*

The only difference in radiance and vibrancy between believers is their service levels. When service to God is the platform one performs on, God will make such a one a Jewel. Anytime service is left off the table, grace and favor are given up and forsaken. In Exodus 19:5, God told Israel *"...if ye will obey my voice indeed, and keep my covenant, then ye shall be a **peculiar treasure** unto me above all people: for all the earth is mine."*

MANTLE FOR THE BATTLE

One of the mantles worn by the last day Church is the mantle of service. Jesus describes an individual in

Luke 12:36 who "...*wait*(s) *for their lord, when he will return from the wedding; that when he cometh and knocketh, they may open unto him immediately.*"

He goes on to add, in Luke 12:37-38, that "*blessed are those **servants**, whom the lord when he cometh shall find watching: verily I say unto you, that he shall gird himself, and make them to sit down to meat, and will come forth and **serve** them. And if he shall come in the second watch, or come in the third watch, and find them so, blessed are those **servants**.*"

These ones are those Jesus called a "*...faithful and wise steward, whom his lord shall make ruler over his household, to give them their portion of meat in due season*" (Luke 12:42). These ones are distinguished from the crowd, and set apart for crowning, because of the mantle of service upon their lives.

They choose to serve, instead of be served and edify the brethren instead of "*...beat(ing) the menservants and maidens, and...eat(ing) and drink(ing), and to be drunken*" (Luke 12:45). As a result of their faithfulness, wisdom and service they were rewarded with grace and favor. They were promoted, blessed, and served by the Master for their kingdom service.

The mantle of service was what differentiated Elisha from the other sons of the prophet. While he "*... poured water on the hands of Elijah*" (2 Kings 3:11), they lounged and gossiped about events (2 Kings 2:3,5). Eventually, Elisha received the mantle of the double-portion for the battle and after parting the river Jordan, the sons of the prophet submitted themselves unto him (2 Kings 3:14-15).

BROKEN SILENCE, AND BREAKTHROUGH SOLUTIONS!

Jason and Ann Beiler (of *Annie pretzels* fame) were youth pastors at a local Church in Pennsylvania, USA when the greatest tragedy of their lives took place. Their second daughter was crushed under a tractor driven by Ann's sister, and died immediately. Their grieving process was abrupt, and none of them had any time to speak to anyone about their inner hurts.

With no one to open up to, Ann reached out to her pastor. In her vulnerable state, he took advantage of her and therein started a six year intimate relationship with the senior pastor of the Church. After fifteen other women in the Church – including two of her sisters and daughter – reported being abused by the senior pastor, Ann confessed to her husband. Jason, expecting him to divorce her.

Instead Jason told her *"Hon, I want you to be happy, and I knew that you weren't happy, but I thought it was because Angie died. I'll do whatever it takes for you to be happy. If you need to go away, if you need to find another place, then just tell me, don't leave a note on the dresser in the middle of the night, but just tell me, and then I'll help you find a place and I'll help you pack your bags, and we'll do it together,"* but he said, *"I just want you to know that if you go, you have to take the girls with you."*

The fact that Jason trusted her with the girls broke her. She was determined then to make her relationship with Jason work and she financially supported him when he decided to go into the new profession of psychology by opening a pretzel shop. After tinkering with the menu a bit, she developed a recipe for pretzels that was much sought after and within 15 years had thousands of branches and more than a billion dollars in revenue.

She credits the power of confession with saving her life, marriage and family. As a result, she started Broken Silence in 2018 with a mission of teaching and equipping women about living a lifestyle of confession that leads to freedom. Today, she and her husband live in Soldano, Texas and have two daughters and six grandchildren. She spoke out the truth of God's word and became an evidence of *gracing favor* in her generation.

Prayer: Mantle of service, fall upon me, in Jesus name.

The Zoe life of God is part of the favored life!

—Tobe Momah M.D.

CHAPTER TWENTY-SIX

SHED LOVE

> *"...hope maketh not ashamed; because the **love of God** is shed abroad in our hearts by the Holy Ghost which is given unto us"* (Romans 5:5).

In the early Church, there was an avalanche of favor, and it was a product of the love they had for God and for one another. In Acts 2:42-46, the Bible says the disciples *"...continued stedfastly in the apostles' doctrine and fellowship, and in breaking of bread, and in prayers* (so that their) *fear came upon every soul and many wonders and signs were done by the apostles. And all that believed were together, and had all things common; And sold their possessions and goods, and parted them to all men, as every man had need. And they, continuing daily with one accord in the temple, and breaking bread from house to house, did eat their meat with gladness and singleness of heart, Praising God, and having **favor with all** the people."*

Where ever love is uncompromising and unashamed, Favor in unstoppable proportions is released.

Unfortunately, the corollary is also possible. The wise man, in NKJV, said, *"an evil man seeks only rebellion; Therefore a cruel messenger will be sent against him.... and whoever rewards evil for good, evil will not depart from his house"* (Proverbs 17:11,13).

There are events of disfavor that are hinged on cruelty, disloyalty, and rebellion. Where love is available, however, favor is unprecedented! In Proverbs 8:21, the wise man says *"I...cause those that love me to inherit substance; and I will fill their treasures"* and in Proverbs 11:16-17, he adds *"a **gracious** woman retaineth honour: and strong men retain riches. The merciful man doeth good to his own soul: but he that is cruel troubleth his own flesh."*

RABID REJOICING, AND POWER PRAISE!

The Psalmist dropped the golden gauntlet for releasing the anointing for *gracing favor* in Psalm 5:11-12. He said, *"...let all those that put their trust in thee rejoice: let them ever shout for joy, because thou defendest them: let them also that **love** thy name be joyful in thee. For thou, LORD, wilt bless the righteous; with **favor** wilt thou compass him as with a shield."*

The secret to grace and favor is a trio of joy, righteousness, and a love relationship with the father. It is verified by the use of the word *for*, as used in Psalm 5:12, and it shows that no true favor operates without a platform of love and loyalty undergirding it. In Psalm 112:5,9, the Psalmist said *"a good man shews favor, and lendeth...He hath dispersed, he hath given to the poor; his righteousness endures for ever...."*

Even Jesus saw increase in the favor and grace upon His life because he Loved God. In Luke 2:49-52, the Bible says Jesus asked his mother "*...wist ye not that I must be about my Father's business?...And Jesus increased in wisdom and stature, and in **favor with God and man**.*"

A love for God, and a hunger to be about the father's business is proof of love for God (John 14:21), and a sure recipe for favor and grace. The God who starts must also finish, and the proof of your finishing is entering through the gates. The two-leaved gates of grace and favor (Isaiah 43:1-3), are open to those who obey willingly and love unabashedly.

Beware of Scoffers!

Scoffers are the scourge of the last day Church! In 2 Peter 3:3-4, the Apostle Peter said "*knowing this first, that there shall come in the last days scoffers, walking after their own lusts, and saying, where is the promise of his coming? for since the fathers fell asleep, all things continue as they were from the beginning of the creation.*"

These ones are insincere and they forsake the truth. In Proverbs 3:3-4, the wise man said "*let not **mercy and truth** forsake thee: bind them about thy neck; write them upon the table of thine heart: So shalt thou find favor and good understanding in the sight of God and man.*"

Those who lack mercy and truth, like scoffers, will miss the end time grace and favor God is pouring out on the world. Without this duo, futility and frustration is inevitable. There must, therefore, be an unlimited mercy without untold truth to crown the Church with His Gracing favor.

In 1 Corinthians 5:7-8, the apostle Paul chides the Corinth Church to "*purge out therefore the old leaven, that ye may be a new lump, as ye are unleavened. For even Christ our passover is sacrificed for us: Therefore let us keep the feast, not with old leaven, neither with the leaven of malice and wickedness; but with the unleavened bread of sincerity and truth.*"

Wherever there is sincerity and truth, there is a feast but where there is malice and wickedness there is famine. What you can become is limited by the sincerity and love you did it with! In 1 Corinthians 9:17, the Bible says "*… if I do this thing willingly, I have a reward: but if against my will, a dispensation of the gospel is committed unto me.*"

APOSTLE OF SIMPLE FAITH, EXPONENT OF THE SPIRIT-FILLED LIFE

Samuel Morris (1872 – 1893) was a Liberian Christian, considered a Christian mystique by some in his time. He was born to pagan parents, who were chieftains in the tribe of Kru. In his teen years, his tribe lost a tribal war, and as a result he was kidnapped and kept imprisoned under tortuous circumstances.

As his health declined, he was one night visited by a bright light that spoke to him telling him to run into the jungle. He followed the light, and ended up at a plantation owned by Methodist Missionaries in Liberia. He was taught to pray, and after hearing the story of Saul's dramatic conversion on the road to Damascus he gave his life to Jesus Christ.

After learning from the missionaries in Liberia, that a certain Rev. Merritt could enlighten him further on salvation and the Holy Spirit, Samuel decided to go to New York. In 1880, he got on a ship to New York from Liberia and ministered powerfully while on the ship, so that many of the crew gave their lives to Christ.

He impacted several lives in New York, but especially at his Sunday school class. As a result, they raised the money needed for him to go to Taylor college in Indiana. While there, he itinerantly preached the gospel in the surrounding area and revolutionized their perception of the spiritual life with his spontaneous preaching and praying.

In 1893, Samuel Norris developed what looked like a Respiratory condition and died. He left such a mark on the University that the University named a residence hall after him. He also impacted many of the students in missions, and spurred an increased participation of the University in sending missionaries to Africa.

Prayer: Let the love of God be shed from my heart, O Lord, to everyone in Jesus name.

When time is coming to an end, time becomes exceptionally important!

—Tobe Momah M.D.

CHAPTER TWENTY-SEVEN

SWIFTNESS

> *"O satisfy us early with thy mercy; that we may rejoice and be glad all our days. Make us glad according to the days wherein thou hast afflicted us, and the years wherein we have seen evil. Let thy work appear unto thy servants, and thy glory unto their children. And let the beauty of the LORD our God be upon us: and establish thou the work of our hands upon us; yea, the work of our hands establish thou it"* (Psalm 90:14-17).

Before a collision of Grace and favor occurs, there must be early mercy or swift obedience in the Church. The last day Church will be birthed on the twin wings of **swiftness** and **strength,** for God *"...will finish the work, and cut it short in righteousness: because a short work will the Lord make upon the earth"* (Romans 9:28).

In Psalm 90:14-17, the Psalmist prayed "...*satisfy us early with thy **mercy**; that we may rejoice and be glad all our days. Make us glad according to the days wherein thou hast afflicted us, and the years wherein we have seen evil. Let thy work appear unto thy servants, and thy **glory** unto their children and let the beauty of the LORD our God be upon us.*"

It is His early mercy that decorates the believer with divine glory and beauty! You may have achieved things in the past, but it will be swifter now than it has ever been. A Church that are swift to obey, will be strong and shine forth. They are the "*...glorious Church...*" spoken about in Ephesians 5:27 that Jesus will come back for in the last days.

SPIRIT OF ACCELERATION

In Romans 9:27-28, "*Esaias...crieth concerning Israel, (that) though the number of the children of Israel be as the sand of the sea, a remnant shall be saved: For he will finish the work, and cut it short in righteousness: because a short work will the Lord make upon the earth.*"

The glorious Church that Jesus is coming for (see Ephesians 5:27), is predicated on a swiftness of divine activity due to human obedience to divine commands. Before the glory or divine favor comes, however, there must be a transfer from the slow lane to the fast lane of the last days.

In Amos 9:13-14, the prophet Amos said "*...the days come, saith the LORD, that the plowman shall overtake the reaper, and the treader of grapes him that soweth seed; and the mountains shall drop sweet wine, and all the hills shall melt. And I will bring again the captivity of my people* *of Israel, and they shall build the waste cities, and inhabit them;...."*

HIS WORDS RUN SWIFTLY!

One of the secrets to favor is swift obedience to the Word of God. In Proverbs 8:33-35, the wise man said *"Hear instruction, and be wise, and refuse it not. Blessed is the man that heareth me, watching daily at my gates, waiting at the posts of my doors. For whoso **findeth** me **findeth** life, and shall obtain **favor** of the LORD."*

The Hebrew word used for **find** in *"...findeth me..."* is the word *Metsa*, which means to *occur* and *meet as present*. It means don't move until God shows up, but when He does, move and pursue Him and you will see life and favor cover your life!

In Proverbs 3:34-35, the wise man said God *"...giveth **grace** unto the lowly* (for) *the wise shall inherit **glory**: but shame shall be the promotion of fools."* The grace of God is the same Greek word, *Charis*, as favor, and it follows the wise (or doers of His word) and is absent in the midst of fools.

GOD'S STOREHOUSE, WITHOUT MAN'S SCHEMES!

My wife and I moved to the United Kingdom (UK) in 2003, few months after our participation in our nation's National Youth Service Corps (NYSC). I headed to the University of London's London School of Hygiene and Tropical Medicine (LSHTM) for post-graduate course work thanks to my family who facilitated the move by providing tuition and accommodation fees throughout the duration of our stay.

On arrival in London, UK my wife and I were pilloried by friends and relatives on the non-feasibility of our "faith" venture. They claimed that as a newly married couple who stepped out without proven sources of income, we were foolhardy and our mission untenable. They were non abating in their tirades, but yet we persisted.

In conversations with my lovely wife during that time, I told her what God had told me in the secret place. He told me, on our arrival in the UK, that He would raise our union to become a storehouse for our respective families and a place where they could receive nourishment.

While my wife worked as a phlebotomist in Colchester, United Kingdom, I worked as a locum Certified Nurse Assistant (CNA) and a multiple products marketer in order to supplement our income during school holidays. There were opportunities to make a *quick dollar* or circumvent the system, but we didn't take any.

In the midst of our financial travails, God spoke and told me to invest almost two thousand dollars to take the Clinical Skills assessment (CSA) exam in Atlanta, USA. I had taken the other three tests needed to become a licensed Physician in the United States of America (USA), and passing this exam would make me eligible for a job in USA. I obeyed, travelled to Atlanta, Georgia USA and God gave me resounding success.

Fourteen years later, my wife and I are substantial investors in the *family project* and God has graciously blessed us to be a source of succor to several projects worldwide. I am, at present, a board certified fellow of the American Academy of Family Physicians and Associate professor at an Academic medical center in Jackson, Mississippi.

Our annual missions' outreach to local areas in Africa feeds, clothes and enables medical attention to reach thousands in some of the most needy communities. Through the grace of God, my wife and I have been empowered by God to change our generation. We, however, don't depend on the schemes of the world, but on His heavenly wisdom which *"if any of you lack…let him ask of God, that giveth to all men liberally, and upbraideth not and it shall be given him"* (James 1:5).

Prayer: Baptize me, O Lord, with the spirit of swift obedience in Jesus name!

The price for insincerity is insecurity!

—Tobe Momah M.D.

CHAPTER TWENTY-EIGHT

SINCERITY

> *"I have given you a land for which ye did not labor, and cities which ye built not, and ye dwell in them; of the vineyards and oliveyards which ye planted not do ye eat. Now therefore fear the LORD, and serve him in **sincerity** and in truth: and put away the gods which your fathers served on the other side of the flood, and in Egypt; and serve ye the LORD* (Joshua 24:13-14).

In 2 Corinthians 1:12, apostle Paul says "*...our rejoicing is this, the testimony of our conscience, that in **simplicity and godly sincerity**, not with fleshly wisdom, but by the **grace** of God, we have had our conversation in the world, and more abundantly to you-ward.*" It was the sincerity and simplicity of their testimony that birthed abundant grace for outward manifestations.

The sister of the wise man in Songs of Solomon was sincere and as a result saw plenty of silver and showers of favor. In S.O.S 8:9, the wise man said, about his sister, that *"if she be a wall, we will build upon her a palace of silver."* To this assertion, she replied *"I am a wall, and my breasts like towers: then was I in his eyes as one that found favor"* (S.O.S 8:10).

The wall, spoken of in S.O.S 8:8:9-10 concerning the wise man's sister, represents straightforward, sincere, and upright living. On the contrary, the wise man said *"...if she be a door, we will inclose her with boards of cedar"* (S.O.S 8:9b). The door represents wavering opinions, and a convoluted thought process that leads to a boarded-up and crippled life.

Transparency: Key to the Turnaround

Your transparency makes for your turnaround, while your isolationism triggers internal strife that eventually consumes you. When the sixty eight sons of Gideon were killed through the conspiracy of their brother Abimelech (see Judges 9:1-5), the brother who escaped (Jotham) called the men of Shechem and Abimelech out for their insincerity.

In Judges 9:19-20, he said *"if ye then have dealt truly and **sincerely** with Jerubbaal and with his house this day, then rejoice ye in Abimelech, and let him also rejoice in you: But if not, let fire come out from Abimelech, and devour the men of Shechem, and the house of Millo; and let fire come out from the men of Shechem, and from the house of Millo, and devour Abimelech."*

Due to their insincerity, it was a matter of time before their conspiracy bedeviled the men of Shechem and Abimelech. In three years, the Bible says *"God sent an* *evil spirit between Abimelech and the men of Shechem; and the men of Shechem dealt **treacherously** with Abimelech: That the cruelty done to the threescore and ten sons of Jerubbaal might come, and their blood be laid upon Abimelech their brother, which slew them; and upon the men of Shechem, which aided him in the killing of his brethren"* (Judges 9:23-24).

The Men of Shechem killed Abimelech, while Abimelech burnt down the city of Shechem (see Judges 9:52-54) because they walked in insincerity that bade an evil spirit of disfavor between both parties. **The insincere relationship is the most important threat to favor in a believers life.** When there is a lack of sincerity between a couple or group of individuals, it affects their grace and favor quotient.

THE GRACE OF LIFE

In 1 Peter 3:7, apostle Peter said *"…ye husbands, dwell with them according to knowledge, giving honor unto the wife, as unto the weaker vessel, and as being heirs together of the **grace of life**; that your prayers be not hindered."* **The grace of life is triggered by sincerity not insincerity.** Those who love sincerely make forceful life advances, while the insincere remain inconsequential in the schemes of life.

In 2 Cor 6:1-6, Apostle Paul charged the Corinth Church saying, I *"…beseech you also that ye receive not the **grace of God** in vain. (For he saith, I have heard thee in a **time accepted**, and in the day of salvation have I succoured thee: behold, now is the **accepted time**; behold, now is the day of salvation.) …But in all **things approving ourselves** as the ministers of God, …by the Holy Ghost, by **love unfeigned**."*

There is a grace that approves you for all things, and makes your time acceptable. It is not taking the Grace of God in vain, and by love unfeigned! Those who love unconditionally and with sincerely, live pure lives that no devil can corrupt. In 1 Peter 1:22-23, apostle Peter says *"...ye have purified your souls in obeying the truth through the Spirit unto unfeigned love of the brethren,... (by) being born again not of corruptible seed, but of incorruptible, by the word of God, which liveth and abideth for ever."*

FLEEING JEZEBEL IN NSUKKA

On a particular Sunday afternoon in 1998, I had been invited to the "mother" campus of the University of Nigeria, in Nsukka, to moderate the final year graduation ceremony of the Christian Union, University of Nigeria, Nsukka Campus. After a great time in God's presence, I asked to be taken to the bus park to catch a bus back to Enugu.

The reason was I had classes the next morning, and even though we had finished late in the evening, I wanted to make an attempt to get to Enugu (the sister campus of the University of Nigeria) that night. My attempts were, however, futile because by the time I got to the bus park the last bus to Enugu had left.

I asked my gracious host to take me to the Nsukka-Enugu expressway, as I felt confident I could flag down, embark, and utilize any Enugu bound vehicle or bus to my destination. Unfortunately, that night was not one of those nights. No one stopped, or the vehicles were full, and at that stretch of road called *Obolla Ofor* I decided to find a hotel to lay my head for the night.

My intention was to sleep a few hours and leave as early as possible. I found a dingy looking hotel, off the main road, paid for a room and crashed. Exhausted, I did not care about the lack of amenities or the worn out furniture in the room. I just wanted to sleep, and thought the staff in the hotel were also that inclined. I was wrong!

At about 2 am, the front door of my room received a loud thud. It was the receptionist who had checked me in a few hours before. A light-skinned and attractive figure, she had cut the impression of a disinterested staffer who was only there for the money. She was speaking in hushed, but very audible tones. She pointedly asked, *do you want any services for the night?* I replied, *No*, and then she added, *do you want my company for the night?*

I was aghast. She began to open the door, and I flew out of my bed and pushed the rickety looking table in my room against the door and began to rebuke the devil. Even though I was twenty five years old, and steaming with testosterone I knew enough of the Word of God to avoid, not allow, the strange woman. Though I knew no one there, and no one knew me there, and some would adjudicate that I could get away with it, I knew the inerrant Word of God that says "*be sure, your sure sin will find you out*" (Numbers 32:23).

I slept with one eye awake, after that, and at the break of dawn I bolted like a gazelle out of the hotel in search of a vehicle to Enugu. I eventually found one, and as I travelled back to my base I wondered how many had fallen for this hotel's front desk harlotry. Truly, the wise man was right. He said, in Proverbs 7:25-27, "*let not thine heart decline to her* (the harlot) *ways, go not astray in her paths. For she hath cast down many wounded: yea, many strong men have been slain by her. Her house is the way to hell, going down to the chambers of death."*

Prayer: Baptize me with the incorruptible seed of your Word, in Jesus name!

Until there is a flavor to your life, you have no favor to dish out!

—Tobe Momah M.D.

CHAPTER TWENTY-NINE

STIRRINGS

> "...*if the Spirit of him that raised up Jesus from the dead dwell in you, he that raised up Christ from the dead shall also* **quicken** *your mortal bodies by his Spirit that dwelleth in you*" (Romans 8:11).

The stir is only as stimulating as its source! If the source of the stir is the Word of God, or the Spirit of God, there are no limits to what possibilities or potentials can be unraveled and shown to the ends of the earth in terms of *gracing favor*.

In Psalm 119:133-135, the Psalmist prayed "*order my steps in thy word: and let not any iniquity have dominion over me. Deliver me from the oppression of man: so will I keep thy precepts. Make thy face to shine upon thy servant; and teach me thy statutes.*"

When God's face shines upon an individual, it is a guarantee of His Grace and favor upon them. Its continuance, however, in contingent of walking by His

Word. In Number 6:25-26, the Lord asked Moses to pray thus upon the children of Israel saying "*the* L*ORD* make his face shine upon thee, and be gracious unto thee (and) *the* L*ORD* lift up his countenance upon thee, and give thee peace."

The face of God shining upon an individual is tantamount to grace and favor. Never let His presence go, but keep pressing in and pursuing God and his grace and favor will always accompany you.

DAY OF WONDERS

The people of Israel left Egypt under the cloud of God's gracing favor! In Exodus 12:36, "…*the* L*ORD* gave the people **favor** *in the sight of the Egyptians, so that they lent unto them such things as they required. And they spoiled the Egyptians.*" They left Egypt with so much silver and gold, that their wealth was trans-generational (see Exodus 3:21-22).

The reason for this uncanny favor, before their avowed enemies, was the hand of God. In Acts 13:17, the Bible says "*the God of this people of Israel chose our fathers, and exalted the people when they dwelt as strangers in the land of Egypt, and with an **high arm** brought he them out of it.*"

The word used to translate *high arm* from the original Greek is the Greek word *Hupselos* and it means to highly esteem, exalt or be lofty. God stirred up the people of Israel, and favor was their outcome. That singular touch from God signaled the favor to transfer wealth, and grace to get out of a life savaged by servitude.

FLAVORED AND FAVORED

Every individual has a choice of who or what stirs Him or her. A believer must, however, be stirred by the Holy Ghost to live a triumphant life. In Romans 8:11, the Bible says that "*if the Spirit of him that raised up Jesus from the dead dwell in you, he that raised up Christ from the dead shall also quicken your mortal bodies by his Spirit that dwelleth in you*" (Romans 8:11).

Jesus was quickened by the power of the Holy Spirit back to life, and so can you and I! If the Holy Spirit's stir could take Jesus from Hell to the highest heights of power, there is no limit to what and where the stir of His power can take you. It can turn your shame to shining, and your garbage to glory.

In Psalm 112:4, the Psalmist said_"*a good man sheweth **favor**, and lendeth: he will guide his affairs with discretion. Surely he shall not be moved forever: the righteous shall be in everlasting remembrance. He shall not be afraid of evil tidings: his heart is fixed, trusting in the* LORD. *His heart is established, he shall not be afraid, until he see his desire upon his enemies.*"

Only a man who is steadfast in faith, and is guided by discretion, can show favor. **Until there is a flavor to your life, you have no favor to dish out**! *Gracing favor* is not a human attribute, but a divine catalyst for unsurpassed greatness, and until the stirring of the Holy Spirit comes upon an individual he or she cannot partake or partner with the Holy Ghost.

RAPID REPAIR BY THE REDEEMER!

The surgeon had just told Rev. Ashbrook, the then District Superintendent of the Louisiana District of the Assemblies of God that he had less than six months to live because he had an inoperable lung mass that with the best of treatment would prolong his life for at most six months to a year. In that one moment, the revered gentleman and his wife faced down the surgeon and told him that in the absence of a cure from medicine or surgery they would depend on God for his healing.

That diagnosis was in the 1960's! Rev. Ashbrook lived another forty years pastoring megachurches from Hong Kong to Louisiana without missing a step. Even though his faith was severely challenged on several occasions, he never quit. His son John remembers him, a times, as been sickly and weak while preaching, but nevertheless kept preaching till he ended his sermon.

Rev. Ashbrook discovered a pivotal scripture that changed his health forever. He was preaching one day from Romans 8:11; and while preaching his sermon, God showed him that the Holy Spirit in him could do what he needed – quicken his mortal body! That scripture says, *"But if the Spirit of him that raised up Jesus from the dead dwell in you, he that raised up Christ from the dead shall also quicken your mortal bodies by his Spirit that dwelleth in you."*

He lifted up his arms in surrender and began to claim that promise for his physical body. After the service, his body was restored by the quickening power of the Holy Spirit and he went on finish his term successfully as the Louisiana State Assemblies of God District Superintendent.

After he retired, he served as the senior pastor of an International Assemblies of God Church in Hong Kong and covered a missionary who was on furlough for a year by serving in Mongolia. At the time of his passing at nearly eighty years of age, he had proven the Word of God. His was a healing life! He walked where others feared to thread and accomplished more than legions of ordinary men do in their lifetimes.

Prayer: I receive Holy Ghost stirs in my spirit man, O Lord, in Jesus name!

***If they can't take it off Jesus,
they can't put it on you!***

—Bishop David Ibiyeomie
Salvation Ministries,
Port Harcourt, Nigeria.

PART IV

CONCLUSION

- **The A to Z of Gracing Favor**

CHAPTER THIRTY

The A to Z of Gracing Favor

> "*He that saith unto the wicked, Thou are righteous; him shall the people curse, nations shall abhor him: But to them that rebuke him shall be delight, and a good blessing shall come upon them. **Every man shall kiss his lips that giveth a right answer**"* (Proverbs 24:24-26).

In an age where hypocrisy is now an art, and the praise of men is exalted above the praise of God (John 12:43), the message of **Gracing Favor** seeks to pierce through the façade. It calls for the real Church to awaken, and show the truth in transparency, honesty and sincerity.

Until the Church goes back to sincerity and truth, the gospel of grace and favor would be lost in the soundbites and clichés of a generation. In Songs of Solomon 1:3, the wise man said *"because of the savor of thy good ointments thy name is as ointment poured forth, therefore do the virgins love thee."*

You cannot give what you do not have. If the ointment in a believer is good, the name of Jesus will sweeten that ointment so that the virgins love him or her, but if the ointment is bad, it will stink! The same oil that causes believer's faces to shine (Psalm 104:15), will when contaminated by dead flies "...*send forth a stinking savor....*" (Ecclesiastes 10:1).

PERPETUATING GRACING FAVOR

In Nehemiah 9:22-25, Nehemiah prayed to God saying "...*thou gavest them* (Israel) *kingdoms and nations, and didst divide them into corners: so they possessed the land of Sihon, and the land of the king of Heshbon, and the land of Og king of Bashan. Their children also multipliedst thou as the stars of heaven, and broughtest them into the land, concerning which thou hadst promised to their fathers, that they should go in to possess it. So the children went in and possessed the land, and thou subduedst before them the inhabitants of the land, the Canaanites, and gavest them into their hands, with their kings, and the people of the land, that they might do with them as they would. And they took strong cities, and a fat land, and possessed houses full of all goods, wells digged, vineyards, and oliveyards, and fruit trees in abundance: so they did eat, and were filled, and became fat, and delighted themselves in thy great goodness.*"

From Psalm 44:3, the Bible teaches us that this "...*great goodness*..." the Israelites tasted was as a result of favor. The recurrent trait, however, in Israel's ballad of maladies is they never perpetuated this grace and favor in their lives. Soon after, "...*they were disobedient, and rebelled against thee, and cast thy law behind their backs, and slew thy prophets which testified against them to turn them to thee, and they wrought great provocations. Therefore* (God) *delivered them into the hand of their enemies, who vexed them: and in the time of their trouble, when they cried unto thee,* (God) *heardest them from heaven; and according to thy* **manifold mercies** *thou gavest them* **saviors,** *who saved them out of the hand of their enemies"* (Nehemiah 9:26-28).

Even the saviors and manifold or abundant mercy were not enough to perpetuate Gracing favor in Israel. Nehemiah said "*...after they had rest, they did evil again before thee: therefore leftest thou them in the land of their enemies, so that they had the dominion over them: yet when they returned, and cried unto thee, thou heardest them from heaven; and many times didst thou deliver them according to thy mercies; And testifiedst against them, that thou mightest bring them again unto thy law: yet they dealt proudly, and hearkened not unto thy commandments, but sinned against thy judgments, (which if a man do, he shall live in them;) and withdrew the shoulder, and hardened their neck, and would not hear. Yet many years didst thou forbear them, and testifiedst against them by thy spirit in thy prophets: yet would they not give ear: therefore gavest thou them into the hand of the people of the lands. Nevertheless for thy great mercies' sake thou didst not utterly consume them, nor forsake them; for thou art a* **gracious** *and* **merciful** *God*" (Nehemiah 9:28-31).

The word **merciful** in Nehemiah 9:31 is the Hebrew word *Rachum,* and it can be translated as *compassionate* or *favored.* I believe the only way to perpetuate Gracing favor is to tap into the two leaved gates of God called gracious and merciful (or favoring). Understanding both aspects and combining them will grant a never before apportioned side of God that will birth unparalleled greatness. For too long, many have used the message of grace and favor as just an opportunity to get, but now God is re-iterating that amidst the benefits he would also give us the grace to stand along side the surplus he will unleash upon the Church.

BEWARE OF THE CONSPIRACY THEORY!

Jonathan and David epitomized *Gracing Favor*. In 1 Samuel 20:3, David said to Jonathan "*…thy father certainly knoweth that I have found **grace** in thine eyes;….*" They loved each other with exceeding favor, with David saying "*…thy love to me was wonderful, passing the love of women*" (2 Samuel 1:26).

There was, however, a conspiracy theory sprung by King Saul, Jonathan's father, to spoil this *gracing favor*. In 1 Samuel 20:30-31, King Saul told Jonathan "*…thou son of the perverse rebellious woman, do not I know that thou hast chosen the son of Jesse to thine own confusion, and unto the confusion of thy mother's nakedness? For as long as the son of Jesse liveth upon the ground, thou shalt not be established, nor thy kingdom. Wherefore now send and fetch him unto me, for he shall surely die.*"

Instead of taking his father's bait, Jonathan decided not to muddle the waters of the relationship between him and David. He rejected his father's overtures to kill David, and rather re-assured David saying "*…far be it from thee: for if I knew certainly that evil were determined by my father to come upon thee, then would not I tell it thee?*" (1 Samuel 20:9).

The last days will signal the death knell of trust between individuals, as a preponderance of humanity will be "... *without natural affection, trucebreakers, false accusers, incontinent, fierce, despisers of those that are good, traitors, heady, high minded, lovers of pleasures more than lovers of God*" (2 Timothy 3:3-4). This distrust will serve as a nidus for the blossoming of conspiracy theories against race, sexes, and individuals.

Amidst the rise of distrust, the Church must beware of conspiracy theories that make individuals feel like everyone is against them! To the contrary, He says, in Ephesians 1:6, that "...*He* (God) *hath made us accepted in the beloved.*" If you can bless without envying others, then you can praise without perjury.

I AM COVENANTED!

When I was Nineteen years old, I was a second year medical student at the University of Nigeria, Enugu Campus and as an ardent lover of Jesus Christ, was in pursuit of God anywhere I was. I had been sent home, alongside my classmates, following one of the numerous Academic Staff Union of Universities (ASUU) strikes and, while at home, I was caught in the crossfire of Nigeria's political upheaval.

On June 12th, 1993 the freest and fairest election in Nigeria' history was annulled by the Babangida administration, and the country was seething. To some, it was tottering on collapse, with the Yoruba nation, threatening secession. As my contribution to national cohesion, I decided to go on a 21 day water-only fast for the Nigerian nation.

While on the fast, I had a visitation from Jesus Christ. He commissioned my humble self, according to Psalm 71:18, to *"...show thy strength unto this generation, and thy power to everyone that is to come."* I entered a covenant to be led by His Spirit, and walk by His Word and I have been covenanted to Him ever since! A few weeks after this visitation, Nigeria was miraculously pulled off the brink, and Faith and Power Ministries was born.

Prayer: Change my heart O Lord. Make it ever new, in Jesus name!

<u>The A to Z of Gracing Favor</u>:

I am **A**ccepted in the beloved
I am **B**lessed in all things
I am **C**overed by the Blood of Jesus
I am **D**elivered from all evil
I am **E**mpowered to prosper
I am highly **F**avored
I walk in divine **G**reatness
I receive divine **H**elp
I am God's **I**nkhorn
I receive Supernatural **J**oy
I am a beneficiary of Divine **K**indness
I am God's **L**oaner
I am God's **M**illionaire
I believe **N**othing is impossible
I am born an **O**vercomer
I am a **P**roblem solver
I am a **Q**uestion Answerer
I am a Rabid **R**ejoicer
I am a **S**olution to this world
I am a **T**ormentor to my enemies
I am **U**nder permanent Divine surveillance
I am a candidate for divine **V**isitation
I am a **W**inner always
I am **X**alted daily with God
I will go **Y**onder than my contemporaries
I will reach my **Z**enith, in Jesus Name!

-Tobe Momah M.D.

OTHER BOOKS BY TOBE MOMAH

1. **Tobe Momah**. A General and a gentleman (*biography of General Sam Momah*) –Spectrum books 2003
2. **Tobe Momah.** Between the systems, soul and spirit of man (*a Christian doctors view on sickness and its source*) – Xulon press 2007
3. **Tobe Momah**. Building lasting relationships (a Manual for the complete home) – Xulon press 2006
4. **Tobe Momah.** Metrobiology – *A Study of life in the city* 1ST ed (a Doctor`s Daily Devotional) – Xulon Press 2008
5. **Tobe Momah.** Pregnancy: Pitfalls, Pearls and principles – Westbow Press 2011
6. **Tobe Momah.** Ultimate Harvest: Five F.A.C.T.S on Fruitfulness and how to grow the American Church again – Westbow Press 2012
7. **Tobe Momah.** From Edginess to Eagerness…*taking the Church back to willing service* Westbow Press 2012
8. **Tobe Momah.** Fear no Evil…*by hating evil* – Westbow Press 2013
9. **Tobe Momah.** Fear no Evil…by hating evil: A daily devotional – Westbow Press 2013
10. **Tobe Momah.** HEALING LIVES……*Stories of encouragement and achievement in the midst of sickness* – Westbow Press 2014
11. **Tobe Momah.** STEPS to the altar…*why a chosen generation is living ashamed at the altar* – Westbow Press 2014
12. **Tobe Momah.** Stay In Tune (S.I.T)…*Challenging an always going but Godless culture!* – Advanced Global Publishing 2015

13. **Tobe Momah**. Stay In Tune (S.I.T)...*Living daily in His presence* (A 366-day Devotional) – Advanced Global Publishing 2015
14. **Tobe Momah**. The Death Knell called Depression. Advanced Global Publishing – 2015
15. **Tobe Momah**. Heirs not Helper...*Raising a generation of plunderers, who are not just pleaders*. Advanced Global Publishing – 2015
16. **Tobe Momah.** Loyalty Legends...*living a life of abundance through the anointing*. Westbow Press (2017)
17. **Tobe Momah.** HEALING LIVES (II)...*Stories of encouragement and achievement in the midst of sickness* – Westbow Press (2017)
18. **Tobe Momah.** The Spirit of Acceleration... *rekindling the hope of those sick at heart*! – Christian Faith Publishers (2019)
19. **Tobe Momah.** Assertive Initiative...*the light that darkness cannot comprehend.* West point press (2022).

ABOUT THE AUTHOR

Tobe Momah MD, currently serves as the Vision Co-coordinator of Faith and Power Ministries, a 501c3 organization, with a prayer ministry in Jackson, Mississippi, and Monroe, Louisiana that is focused on building a prayer hedge over these two states and her surrounding environs. In pursuit of his God given vision to *"show His strength to this generation, and His power to all shall come..."* (Psalm 71:18), faith and Power Ministries airs Miracle radio on WNPR 99.1 Mississippi every Wednesday (6:30am – 7am) weekly and *"Health and Wellness with Dr. Tobe"* television programs daily on KMCT 39 Monroe, Louisiana.

This is beside the twice monthly Holy Ghost Night meetings, that hold on the second and last Fridays of each month in Jackson, MS and Monroe LA respectively (between 11pm and 4 am). The ministry also organizes an annual medical missions and through these missions (which have occurred annually between 2012 and 2021), thousands have been saved, healed, and delivered.

Dr Tobe Momah is core faculty and associate professor of Family Medicine at the University of Mississippi Medical Center (UMMC), Jackson USA since arriving Mississippi in 2017. He trained at the University of Nigeria, College of Medicine, Enugu Nigeria - where he served as two time vice president of the

Christian Union campus fellowship - and the University of London, School of Hygiene and tropical medicine where he obtained his medical degree in Medicine/surgery and his Master's in medical parasitology/tropical medicine respectively.

Tobe Momah has more than forty scientific publications and twenty books in print. He attended the family medicine residency at The Brooklyn Hospital center, Weill Cornell Hospital system in New York, and has worked in the private, public and community health sphere prior to entering the academia at UMMC. He has traveled extensively to African nations, including Sierra Leone, Nigeria, Ethiopia, Mozambique on medical missions and provides free medical health care to the residents of that area who require medical help. He is board certified in Family Medicine and obesity Medicine and serves as an associate Pastor at Miracle Temple Evangelistic Church, Jackson MS.

He is married to Rita Momah (a public health specialist) and they are blessed with a set of twins Kingsley and Gloria. They make their home in the Madison, Ms area.

CPSIA information can be obtained
at www.ICGtesting.com
Printed in the USA
BVHW081931060723
666850BV00004B/225

9 781959 895510